In Memory of

Karen Ann Watkins

Granddaughter

of

Jane and Leonard

Frank

LORD BYRON

Selected Poems

LORD BYRON

Selected Poems

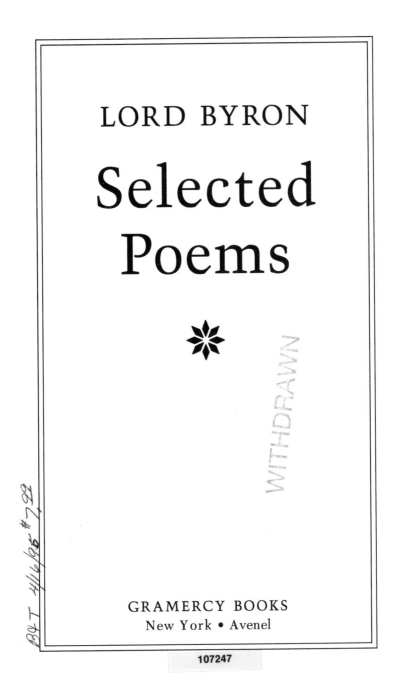

GRAMERCY BOOKS
New York • Avenel

Introduction and compilation
Copyright © 1994 by Random House Value Publishing, Inc.
All rights reserved

This 1994 edition is published by Gramercy Books,
distributed by Random House Value Publishing, Inc.,
40 Engelhard Avenue,
Avenel, New Jersey 07001.

Random House
New York • Toronto • London • Sydney • Auckland

Printed and bound in the United States

Library of Congress Cataloging-in-Publication Data

Byron, George Gordon, Baron 1788-1824
[Selections.]
Lord Byron: selected poems
p.   cm.
ISBN: 0-517-11832-7
I. Title.
PR4353   1994
821'.7—dc20   94-14795   CIP

8 7 6 5 4 3 2 1

CONTENTS

From English Bards and Scotch Reviewers

From Childe Harold's Pilgrimage

The Vision of Judgment

From Don Juan

INTRODUCTION

In nineteenth-century England and Europe, George Gordon, Lord Byron, was considered *the* English Romantic poet. Unlike his contemporaries William Wordsworth and Percy Bysshe Shelley, Byron had an immense reputation in Europe during his lifetime and was considered among the greatest of the British poets—second only to Shakespeare. He greatly influenced such writers as Honoré de Balzac and Johann Wolfgang von Goethe as well as composers like Hector Berlioz and Ludwig van Beethoven. The public considered Byron the personification of his own literary creation, the "Byronic hero," the archetypal romantic protagonist—a moody, passionate, proud, and sexually alluring wanderer who seemed to have stepped out of a dark gothic novel. As the philosopher Bertrand Russell wrote, Byron embodied the essential romantic trait, "Titanic cosmic self-assertion" and his influence over the public imagination was strong even after his death. As Matthew Arnold, the Victorian critic and poet, wrote in 1850, the world "had *felt* him like the thunder's roll."

George Gordon Byron was born in London on January 22, 1788 into a colorful family that traced their ancestry to the time of William the Conqueror. His grandfather was John "Foul-weather Jack" Byron, an admiral in the Royal Navy, who described his adventures of shipwreck and hardship in his book *Narrative*. Byron's father was Captain John "Mad Jack" Byron, a rake and a fortune-hunter. Byron's mother, Catherine Gordon of Gight, Scotland, was the second wife of "Mad Jack" who by the time he died had succeeded in spending both wives' fortunes. He left his family in poverty and Catherine had no choice but to take her three-year-old son to live in Aberdeen.

When Byron was ten there was another reversal of fortune after the death of his reclusive great-uncle. William, known as the "Wicked Lord" ever since he had killed his cousin in a duel, was the fifth Lord Byron. The youngster became the sixth and moved to the family estates in Nottingham.

Byron was born with a club foot and inept medical treatment had made the disability worse. His sensitivity to his lameness made Byron compensate by excelling in athletics, including swimming, boxing, fencing, and horsemanship. When he attended Harrow, the exclusive English school, from 1801-1805, he earned the respect of his schoolmates by pummeling anyone who ridiculed his gait. Byron went on to Trinity College, Cambridge, where he led the life of a dissipated lord. Among his well-known idiosyncracies was the pet bear he kept in the small tower room above his quarters.

Byron was sexually precocious. As he wrote: "My passions were developed very early—so early, that few would believe me, if I were to state the period, and the facts which accompanied it." In his mother's absence, May Gray, a maid in the household, had mistreated the ten-year-old Byron with beatings and neglect in addition to sexual abuse. Among his youthful infatuations was one with Mary Duff, an older distant cousin. Later, at Cambridge, Byron formed his first homosexual liaisons with classmates Edward Long and John Edleston, a choir boy "whom," he wrote, "I loved more than I ever loved a living thing."

After he received his degree in 1808 Byron moved to London where he dabbled in politics since as a baron he inherited a seat in the House of Lords. He also led the life of a young dandy, nobleman, and writer. His first publicly published book of verse was *Hours of Idleness* (1807), made up of short pieces, most of which were written during his Harrow days. It was severely criticized—not unjustly—by the *Edinburgh Review*. This prompted young Byron to write his first major poem, *English Bards and Scotch Reviewers* (1809), a satire in which he takes caustic and humorous aim at contemporary critics and poets—including Wordsworth and Coleridge.

In mid 1809 he left England for a tour through Portugal, Spain, Malta, Albania, Greece, and Asia Minor. His travels became the inspiration for the first two cantos of *Childe Harold's Pilgrimage* that were published two years later. The slim book was a literary sensation whereupon Byron became, quite suddenly, the toast of Regency London. He wrote: "I awoke one morning and found myself famous." The public immediately identified the author with his dark, brooding hero.

Byron was extremely handsome. "So beautiful a countenance I scarcely ever saw," wrote the poet Samuel Taylor Coleridge, ". . . his eyes the open portals of the sun—things of light, and for light." He was literally besieged by women. The eccentric writer Lady Caroline Lamb found Byron to be "mad—bad—and dangerous to know" and launched into frenzied pursuit. And, in 1813, he and his married half sister, Augusta Leigh, embarked upon a passionate affair.

To escape his harried existence and believing marriage was the answer to his problems, in 1815, Byron married Annabella Milbanke; it was soon apparent that the union was ill-matched. A child, Augusta Ada, was born within the year, but the marriage was dissolved soon after when Lady Byron learned of the incestuous relationship between Byron and Augusta. And because of his lavish lifestyle Byron was in dire financial straits; he was deeply in debt despite continuing sales of a series of verse tales—*The Giaour, The Bride of Abydos, The Corsair,* and *Lara*—that he wrote rapidly between 1813 and 1816.

On April 15, 1816, to escape the scandal, Byron left England. For the rest of his life he wandered the Continent in self-imposed exile. In Geneva he began a friendship with Percy Shelley, who was there with his wife Mary Godwin. There, too, he finished the third canto of *Childe Harold's Pilgrimage* and had a brief affair with another ardent and aggressive admirer, Claire Clairmont, Mary's half-sister. A child, Allegra, was born of this liaison.

Byron then moved on to Venice to perhaps his most debauched period as well as the beginning of his most creatively productive; in Italy he finished the fourth canto of *Childe Harold's Pilgrimage,* wrote *The Vision of Judgment* (1822) and the sixteen cantos of *Don Juan,* considered to be his best and most mature works. In addition to his various semi-permanent mistresses, he kept in his rented palazzo an everchanging harem of Venetian women; by Byron's own count there were more than two hundred.

By 1818, Byron tired of his life of promiscuous dissipation. He soon became devoted to the nineteen-year-old Countess Teresa Guiccioli, who was then married to a man thirty-nine years her senior. Through Teresa's family, the Gambas, he also became drawn into the Carbonari movement, the revolutionary struggle against Austrian rule in northern Italy. When the Gambas were exiled to Pisa, in 1821, Byron followed and met Shelley again and became part of a group of friends called the "Pisan Circle." A year later Shelley drowned and Byron was much affected by his death.

Soon afterward Byron became involved in the Greek War of Independence. In late December 1823, he left Italy for Missolonghi, Greece. Despite his own doubts about the unruly factions involved in the Greek struggle against the Turks, Byron spent his own money for supplies to outfit troops.

In the end he gave his life to the cause. Amid an intense electrical storm, after repeated and harmful bleedings, Byron died of a fever on April 19, 1824. He was thirty-six years old. Ironically, his death did more for the success of the revolution than any of his own efforts and Byron is still revered as a Greek national hero.

Unlike many other poets, Byron lived an eventful and public life and, accordingly, his verse focuses upon the factual world and rarely strays into metaphysics or abstractions. After Chaucer, Byron is one of the greatest writers of narrative poetry in English. A marvelous storyteller, his best verse is marked by spontaneity and a natural and colloquial style that are among his hallmarks. Another is his sense of humor. Byron said, "There are but two sentiments to which I am constant—a strong love of liberty, and a detestation of cant," and he enjoyed poking through the hypocrisy and complacency of the establishment. In one of his greatest poems, *The Vision of Judgment*, he hilariously satirizes the late King George III by describing quite blasphemously, his surreptitious entry into heaven. *Don Juan*, Byron's masterpiece, was, as he wrote, "a *satire* on the *abuses* of the present state of society." Amid declamations of licentiousness and blasphemy, he upheld it to be "the most moral of poems; but if people won't discover the moral, that it their fault, not mine." Unlike the reprehensible Don Juan of legend, Byron's Juan is an innocent youth who is "more sinned against than sinning," and encounters through his picaresque travels the evil and corruption of the world.

At its best Byron's poetry has a vitality and exuberance that reflects his effort to portray life honestly. Byron himself wrote a fitting assessment of his achievement and contribution to English poetry in a letter to a friend. Speaking of *Don Juan* he said, "it is the sublime of *that there* sort of writing—it may be bawdy . . . but is it not *life*, is it not *the thing?*—Could any man have written it—who has not lived in the world?"

This collection contains a selection of Byron's best shorter lyric works, including such famous poems as "She Walks in Beauty," "So We'll Go No More A-Roving," and "When We Two Parted." *The Vision of Judgment*, one of his major longer poems, is included in its entirety. And there are excerpts from *Childe Harold's Pilgrimage* and *Don Juan*.

CHRISTOPHER MOORE

New York
1994

Lyric Poems

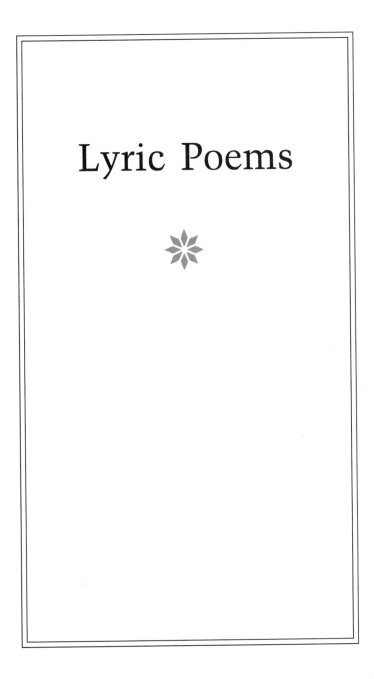

A FRAGMENT

When, to their airy hall, my fathers' voice,
Shall call my spirit, joyful in their choice;
When, pois'd upon the gale, my form shall ride,
Or, dark in mist, descend the mountain's side;
Oh! may my shade behold no sculptur'd urns,
To mark the spot, where earth to earth returns:
No lengthen'd scroll, no praise encumber'd stone;
My epitaph shall be, my name alone:
If *that* with honor fail to crown my clay,
Oh! may no other fame my deeds repay,
That, only *that,* shall single out the spot,
By that remember'd, or with that forgot.

ON A DISTANT VIEW OF THE VILLAGE
AND SCHOOL OF HARROW ON THE HILL

Oh! mihi praeteritos referat si Jupiter annos.

Virgil

Ye scenes of my childhood, whose loved recollection
 Embitters the present, compared with the past;
Where science first dawned on the powers of reflection,
 And friendships were formed, too romantic to last;

Where fancy, yet, joys to trace the resemblance
 Of comrades, in friendship and mischief allied;
How welcome to me your ne'er fading remembrance,
 Which rests in the bosom, though hope is denied!

Again I revisit the hills where we sported,
 The streams where we swam, and the fields where we
  fought;
The school where, loud warned by the bell, we resorted,
 To pore o'er the precepts by pedagogues taught.

Again I behold where for hours I have pondered,
 As reclining, at eve, on yon tombstone I lay;
Or round the steep brow of the churchyard I wandered,
 To catch the last gleam of the sun's setting ray.

I once more view the room, with spectators surrounded,
 Where, as Zanga, I trod on Alonzo o'erthrown;
While, to swell my young pride, such applauses resounded,
 I fancied that Mossop himself was outshone:

Or, as Lear, I poured forth the deep imprecation,
 By my daughters, of kingdom and reason deprived;

Till, fired by loud plaudits and self-adulation,
  I regarded myself as a Garrick revived.

Ye dreams of my boyhood, how much I regret you!
  Unfaded your memory dwells in my breast;
Though sad and deserted, I ne'er can forget you:
  Your pleasures may still be in fancy possessed.

To Ida full oft may remembrance restore me,
  While fate shall the shades of the future unroll!
Since darkness o'ershadows the prospect before me,
  More dear is the beam of the past to my soul.

But if, through the course of the years which await me,
  Some new scene of pleasure should open to view,
I will say, while with rapture the thought shall elate me,
  "Oh! such were the days which my infancy knew!"

DAMAETAS

In law an infant, and in years a boy,
In mind a slave to every vicious joy,
From every sense of shame and virtue wean'd,
In lies an adept, in deceit a fiend;
Vers'd in hypocrisy, while yet a child,
Fickle as wind, of inclinations wild;
Woman his dupe, his heedless friend a tool,
Old in the world, though scarcely broke from school;
Damaetas ran through all the maze of sin,
And found the goal, when others just begin:
Ev'n still conflicting passions shake his soul,
And bid him drain the dregs of pleasure's bowl;
But, pall'd with vice, he breaks his former chain,
And, what was once his bliss, appears his bane.

BRIGHT BE THE PLACE OF THY SOUL

Bright be the place of thy soul!
  No lovelier spirit than thine
E'er burst from its mortal control,
  In the orbs of the blessed to shine.

On earth thou wert all but divine,
  As thy soul shall immortally be;
And our sorrow may cease to repine,
  When we know that thy God is with thee.

Light be the turf of thy tomb!
  May its verdure like emeralds be:
There should not be the shadow of gloom
  In aught that reminds us of thee.

Young flowers and an evergreen tree
  May spring from the spot of thy rest:
But nor cypress nor yew let us see;
  For why should we mourn for the blessed?

WHEN WE TWO PARTED

1

When we two parted
In silence and tears,
Half brokenhearted
To sever for years,
Pale grew thy cheek and cold,
Colder thy kiss;
Truly that hour foretold
Sorrow to this.

2

The dew of the morning
Sunk chill on my brow—
It felt like the warning
Of what I feel now.
Thy vows are all broken,
And light is thy fame;
I hear thy name spoken,
And share in its shame.

3

They name thee before me,
A knell to mine ear;
A shudder comes o'er me—
Why wert thou so dear?
They know not I knew thee,
Who knew thee too well—
Long, long shall I rue thee,
Too deeply to tell.

4

In secret we met—
   In silence I grieve,
That thy heart could forget,
   Thy spirit deceive.
If I should meet thee
   After long years,
How should I greet thee!—
   With silence and tears.

THE FAREWELL TO A LADY

When man expell'd from Eden's bowers,
   A moment linger'd near the gate,
Each scene recall'd the vanish'd hours,
   And bade him curse his future fate.

But wandering on through distant climes,
   He learnt to bear his load of grief;
Just gave a sigh to other times,
   And found in busier scenes relief.

Thus, lady! will it be with me,
   And I must view thy charms no more;
For while I linger near to thee
   I sigh for all I knew before.

In flight I shall be surely wise,
   Escaping from temptation's snare;
I cannot view my Paradise
   Without the wish of dwelling there.

LINES TO MR. HODGSON
WRITTEN ON BOARD THE LISBON PACKET

Huzza! Hodgson, we are going,
  Our embargo's off at last;
Favorable breezes blowing
  Bend the canvas o'er the mast.
From aloft the signal's streaming,
  Hark! the farewell gun is fired;
Women screeching, tars blaspheming,
  Tell us that our time's expired.
    Here's a rascal
    Come to task all,
Prying from the Custom house;
    Trunks unpacking
    Cases cracking,
Not a corner for a mouse
'Scapes unsearched amid the racket,
Ere we sail on board the Packet.

Now our boatmen quit their mooring,
  And all hands must ply the oar;
Baggage from the quay is lowering,
  We're impatient, push from shore.
"Have a care! that case holds liquor—
  Stop the boat—I'm sick—oh Lord!"
"Sick, ma'am, damme, you'll be sicker,
  Ere you've been an hour on board."
    Thus are screaming
    Men and women,
Gemmen, ladies, servants, Jacks;
    Here entangling,
    All are wrangling,
Stuck together close as wax—

Such the general noise and racket,
Ere we reach the Lisbon Packet.

Now we've reached her, lo! the Captain,
    Gallant Kidd, commands the crew;
Passengers their berths are clapped in,
    Some to grumble, some to spew.
"Hey day! call you that a cabin?
Why 'tis hardly three feet square;
Not enough to stow Queen Mab in—
Who the deuce can harbor there?"
    "Who, sir? plenty—
    Nobles twenty
Did at once my vessel fill."—
    "Did they? Jesus,
    How you squeeze us!
Would to God they did so still:
Then I'd scape the heat and racket
Of the good ship, Lisbon Packet."

Fletcher! Murray! Bob! where are you?
    Stretched along the deck like logs—
Bear a hand, you jolly tar, you!
    Here's a rope's end for the dogs.
Hobhouse muttering fearful curses,
    As the hatchway down he rolls,
Now his breakfast, now his verses,
    Vomits forth—and damns our souls.
    "Here's a stanza
    On Braganza—
Help!"—" A couplet?"—" No, a cup
    Of warm water—"
    "What's the matter?"
"Zounds! my liver's coming up;
I shall not survive the racket
Of this brutal Lisbon Packet."

Now at length we're off for Turkey,
    Lord knows when we shall come back!
Breezes foul and tempests murky
    May unship us in a crack,
But, since life at most a jest is,
    As philosophers allow,
Still to laugh by far the best is,
    Then laugh on—as I do now.
        Laugh at all things,
        Great and small things,
    Sick or well, at sea or shore;
        While we're quaffing,
        Let's have laughing—
    Who the devil cares for more?—
Some good wine! and who would lack it,
Ev'n on board the Lisbon Packet?

THE SPELL IS BROKE, THE CHARM IS FLOWN!

WRITTEN AT ATHENS, JANUARY 16, 1810

The spell is broke, the charm is flown!
    Thus is it with life's fitful fever:
We madly smile when we should groan:
    Delirium is our best deceiver.

Each lucid interval of thought
    Recalls the woes of Nature's charter;
And he that acts as wise men ought,
    But lives, as saints have died, a martyr.

WRITTEN AFTER SWIMMING FROM SESTOS TO ABYDOS

If, in the month of dark December,
    Leander, who was nightly wont
(What maid will not the tale remember?)
    To cross thy stream, broad Hellespont!

If, when the wintry tempest roared,
    He sped to Hero, nothing loth,
And thus of old thy current poured,
    Fair Venus! how I pity both!

For *me*, degenerate modern wretch,
    Though in the genial month of May,
My dripping limbs I faintly stretch,
    And think I've done a feat today.

But since he crossed the rapid tide,
    According to the doubtful story,
To woo—and—Lord knows what beside.
    And swam for Love, as I for Glory;

'Twere hard to say who fared the best:
    Sad mortals! thus the Gods still plague you!
He lost his labor, I my jest;
    For he was drowned, and I've the ague.

ONE STRUGGLE MORE, AND I AM FREE

One struggle more, and I am free
    From pangs that rend my heart in twain;
One last long sigh to love and thee,
    Then back to busy life again.
It suits me well to mingle now
    With things that never pleased before:
Though every joy is fled below,
    What future grief can touch me more?

Then bring me wine, the banquet bring;
    Man was not formed to live alone:
I'll be that light, unmeaning thing,
    That smiles with all, and weeps with none.
It was not thus in days more dear,
    It never would have been, but thou
Hast fled, and left me lonely here;
    Thou'rt nothing—all are nothing now.

In vain my lyre would lightly breathe!
    The smile that sorrow fain would wear
But mocks the woe that lurks beneath,
    Like roses o'er a sepulcher.
Though gay companions o'er the bowl
    Dispel awhile the sense of ill;
Though pleasure fires the maddening soul,
    The heart—the heart is lonely still!

On many a lone and lovely night
    It soothed to gaze upon the sky;
For then I deemed the heavenly light
    Shone sweetly on thy pensive eye:

And oft I thought at Cynthia's noon,
  When sailing o'er the Aegean wave,
"Now Thyrza gazes on that moon"—
  Alas, it gleamed upon her grave!

When stretched on fever's sleepless bed,
  And sickness shrunk my throbbing veins.
"'Tis comfort still," I faintly said,
  "That Thyrza cannot know my pains":
Like freedom to the time-worn slave—
  A boon 'tis idle then to give—
Relenting Nature vainly gave
  My life, when Thyrza ceased to live!

My Thyrza's pledge in better days,
  When love and life alike were new!
How different now thou meet'st my gaze!
  How tinged by time with sorrow's hue!
The heart that gave itself with thee
  Is silent—ah, were mine as still!
Though cold as e'en the dead can be,
  It feels, it sickens with the chill.

Thou bitter pledge! thou mournful token!
  Though painful, welcome to my breast!
Still, still, preserve that love unbroken,
  Or break the heart to which thou'rt pressed!
Time tempers love, but not removes,
  More hallowed when its hope is fled:
Oh! what are thousand living loves
  To that which cannot quit the dead?

AND THOU ART DEAD, AS YOUNG AS FAIR

*Heu, quanto minus est cum reliquis versari quam
tui meminisse!*

And thou art dead, as young and fair,
    As aught of mortal birth;
And form so soft, and charms so rare,
    Too soon returned to Earth!
Though Earth received them in her bed,
And o'er the spot the crowd may tread
    In carelessness or mirth,
There is an eye which could not brook
A moment on that grave to look.

I will not ask where thou liest low,
    Nor gaze upon the spot;
There flowers or weeds at will may grow,
    So I behold them not:
It is enough for me to prove
That what I loved, and long must love,
    Like common earth can rot;
To me there needs no stone to tell.
'Tis Nothing that I loved so well.

Yet did I love thee to the last
    As fervently as thou,
Who didst not change through all the past,
    And canst not alter now.
The love where Death has set his seal,
Nor age can chill, nor rival steal,
    Nor falsehood disavow:
And, what were worse, thou canst not see
Or wrong, or change, or fault in me.

The better days of life were ours;
    The worst can be but mine:
The sun that cheers, the storm that lowers,
    Shall never more be thine.
The silence of that dreamless sleep
I envy now too much to weep;
    Nor need I to repine
That all those charms have passed away;
I might have watched through long decay.

The flower in ripened bloom unmatched
    Must fall the earliest prey;
Though by no hand untimely snatched,
    The leaves must drop away:
And yet it were a greater grief
To watch it withering, leaf by leaf,
    Than see it plucked today;
Since earthly eye but ill can bear
To trace the change to foul from fair.

I know not if I could have borne
    To see thy beauties fade;
The night that followed such a morn
    Had worn a deeper shade:
Thy day without a cloud hath passed,
And thou wert lovely to the last;
    Extinguished, not decayed;
As stars that shoot along the sky
Shine brightest as they fall from high.

As once I wept, if I could weep,
    My tears might well be shed,
To think I was not near to keep
    One vigil o'er thy bed;
To gaze, how fondly! on thy face,
To fold thee in a faint embrace,

Uphold thy drooping head;
And show that love, however vain,
Nor thou nor I can feel again.

Yet how much less it were to gain,
    Though thou hast left me free,
The loveliest things that still remain,
    Than thus remember thee!
The all of thine that cannot die
Through dark and dread Eternity
    Returns again to me,
And more thy buried love endears
Than aught, except its living years.

WRITTEN BENEATH A PICTURE

1

Dear object of defeated care!
    Though now of Love and thee bereft,
To reconcile me with despair
    Thine image and my tears are left.

2

'Tis said with Sorrow Time can cope;
    But this I feel can ne'er be true:
For by the death-blow of my Hope
    My Memory immortal grew.

STANZAS FOR MUSIC

O Lachrymarum fons, tenero sacros
Ducentium ortus ex animo: quater
Felix! in imo qui scatentem
Pectore te, pia Nympha, sensit.
Gray's Poemata

1

There's not a joy the world can give like that it takes away,
When the glow of early thought declines in feeling's dull
    decay;
'Tis not on youth's smooth cheek the blush alone, which
    fades so fast,
But the tender bloom of heart is gone, ere youth itself be
    past.

2

Then the few whose spirits float above the wreck of happiness,
Are driven o'er the shoals of guilt or ocean of excess:
The magnet of their course is gone, or only points in vain
The shore to which their shiver'd sail shall never stretch
    again.

3

Then the mortal coldness of the soul like death itself
    comes down;
It cannot feel for others' woes, it dare not dream its own;
That heavy chill has frozen o'er the fountain of our tears,
And tho' the eye may sparkle still, 'tis where the ice
    appears.

4

Tho' wit may flash from fluent lips, and mirth distract the
    breast,
Through midnight hours that yield no more their former
    hope of rest;
'Tis but as ivy leaves around the ruin'd turret wreath,
All green and wildly fresh without but worn and gray
    beneath.

5

Oh could I feel as I have felt—or be what I have been,
Or weep as I could once have wept, o'er many a vanished
    scene:
As springs in deserts found seem sweet, all brackish
    though they be,
So midst the wither'd waste of life, those tears would flow
    to me.

REMEMBER THEE! REMEMBER THEE!

Remember thee! remember thee!
    Till Lethe quench life's burning stream
Remorse and Shame shall cling to thee,
    And haunt thee like a feverish dream!

Remember thee! Aye, doubt it not.
    Thy husband too shall think of thee:
By neither shalt thou be forgot,
    Thou *false* to him, thou *fiend* to me!

ODE TO NAPOLEON BUONAPARTE

Expende Annibalem—quot libras in duce
summo Invenies?—
Juvenal Satire X [147-8]

The Emperor Nepos was acknowledged by the *Senate,*
by the *Italians,* and by the Provincials of *Gaul;* his moral
virtues, and military talents, were loudly celebrated; and
those who derived any private benefit from his govern-
ment, announced in prophetic strains the restoration of
public felicity.

✿ ✿ ✿ ✿ ✿ ✿ ✿ ✿ ✿ ✿ ✿ ✿
✿ ✿ ✿ ✿ ✿ ✿ ✿ ✿ ✿ ✿ ✿ ✿

By this shameful abdication, he protracted his life a few
years, in a very ambiguous state, between an Emperor and
an Exile, till——
Gibbon's Decline and Fall [Chap. 36]

1

'Tis done—but yesterday a King!
And arm'd with Kings to strive—
And now thou art a nameless thing
So abject—yet alive!
Is this the man of thousand thrones,
Who strew'd our Earth with hostile bones,
And can he thus survive?
Since he, miscall'd the Morning Star,
Nor man nor fiend hath fall'n so far.

2

Ill-minded man! why scourge thy kind
Who bow'd so low the knee?

By gazing on thyself grown blind,
   Thou taught'st the rest to see.
With might unquestion'd—power to save—
Thine only gift hath been the grave
   To those that worshipp'd thee;
Nor till thy fall could mortals guess
Ambition's less than littleness!

3

Thanks for that lesson—it will teach
   To after-warriors more
Than high Philosophy can preach,
   And vainly preached before.
That spell upon the minds of men
Breaks never to unite again,
   That led them to adore
Those Pagod things of saber-sway,
With fronts of brass, and feet of clay.

4

The triumph, and the vanity,
   The rapture of the strife—
The earthquake voice of Victory,
   To thee the breath of life;
The sword, the scepter, and that sway
Which man seem'd made but to obey,
   Wherewith renown was rife—
All quell'd!—Dark Spirit! what must be
The madness of thy memory!

5

The Desolator desolate!
   The Victor overthrown!
The Arbiter of other's fate
   A Suppliant for his own!

Is it some yet imperial hope
That with such change can calmly cope?
    Or dread of death alone?
To die a prince—or live a slave—
Thy choice is most ignobly brave!

6

He who of old would rend the oak,
    Dreamed not of the rebound;
Chained by the trunk he vainly broke—
    Alone—how looked he round?
Thou in the sternness of thy strength
An equal deed hast done at length,
    And darker fate hast found:
He fell, the forest-prowlers' prey;
But thou must eat thy heart away!

7

The Roman, when his burning heart
    Was slaked with blood of Rome,
Threw down the dagger—dared depart,
    In savage grandeur, home—
He dared depart in utter scorn
Of men that such a yoke had borne,
    Yet left him such a doom!
His only glory was that hour
Of self-upheld abandon'd power.

8

The Spaniard, when the lust of sway
    Had lost its quickening spell,
Cast crowns for rosaries away,
    An empire for a cell;
A strict accountant of his beads,
A subtle disputant on creeds,

His dotage trifled well:
Yet better had he neither known
A bigot's shrine, nor despot's throne.

9

But thou—from thy reluctant hand
The thunderbolt is wrung—
Too late thou leav'st the high command
To which thy weakness clung;
All Evil Spirit as thou art,
It is enough to grieve the heart,
To see thine own unstrung;
To think that God's fair world hath been
The footstool of a thing so mean;

10

And Earth hath spilt her blood for him,
Who thus can hoard his own!
And Monarchs bowed the trembling limb,
And thanked him for a throne!
Fair Freedom! we may hold thee dear,
When thus thy mightiest foes their fear
In humblest guise have shown.
Oh! ne'er may tyrant leave behind
A brighter name to lure mankind!

11

Thine evil deeds are writ in gore,
Nor written thus in vain—
Thy triumphs tell of fame no more,
Or deepen every stain—
If thou hadst died as honor dies,
Some new Napoleon might arise,
To shame the world again—
But who would soar the solar height,
To set in such a starless night?

12

Weigh'd in the balance, hero dust
    Is vile as vulgar clay;
Thy scales, Mortality! are just
    To all that pass away;
But yet methought the living great
Some higher sparks should animate,
    To dazzle and dismay;
Nor deem'd Contempt could thus make mirth
Of these, the Conquerors of the earth.

13

And she, proud Austria's mournful flower,
    Thy still imperial bride;
How bears her breast the torturing hour?
    Still clings she to thy side?
Must she too bend, must she too share
Thy late repentance, long despair,
    Thou throneless Homicide?
If still she loves thee, hoard that gem,
'Tis worth thy vanished diadem!

14

Then haste thee to thy sullen Isle,
    And gaze upon the sea;
That element may meet thy smile,
    It ne'er was ruled by thee!
Or trace with thine all idle hand
In loitering mood upon the sand
    That Earth is now as free!
That Corinth's pedagogue hath now
Transferred his bye word to thy brow.

15

Thou Timour! in his captive's cage
    What thoughts will there be thine,

While brooding in thy prisoned rage?
But one—"The world *was* mine";
Unless, like he of Babylon,
All sense is with thy scepter gone,
   Life will not long confine
That spirit poured so widely forth—
So long obeyed—so little worth!

16

Or like the thief of fire from heaven,
   Wilt thou withstand the shock?
And share with him, the unforgiven,
   His vulture and his rock!
Foredoomed by God—by man accursed,
And that last act, though not thy worst,
   The very Fiend's arch mock;
He in his fall preserv'd his pride,
And if a mortal, had as proudly died!

STANZAS FOR MUSIC

I speak not—I trace not—I breathe not thy name,
There is grief in the sound—there were guilt in the fame;
But the tear which now burns on my cheek may impart
The deep thought that dwells in that silence of heart.

Too brief for our passion, too long for our peace,
Were those hours, can their joy or their bitterness cease?
We repent—we abjure—we will break from our chain;
We must part—we must fly to—unite it again.

Oh! thine be the gladness and mine be the guilt,
Forgive me adored one—forsake if thou wilt;
But the heart which I bear shall expire undebased,
And man shall not break it—whatever thou may'st.

And stern to the haughty, but humble to thee,
My soul in its bitterest blackness shall be;
And our days seem as swift—and our moments more
    sweet,
With thee by my side—than the world at our feet.

One sigh of thy sorrow—one look of thy love,
Shall turn me or fix, shall reward or reprove;
And the heartless may wonder at all we resign,
Thy lip shall reply not to them—but to mine.

SHE WALKS IN BEAUTY

1

She walks in beauty, like the night
  Of cloudless climes and starry skies;
And all that's best of dark and bright
  Meet in her aspect and her eyes:
Thus mellow'd to that tender light
  Which heaven to gaudy day denies.

2

One shade the more, one ray the less,
  Had half impair'd the nameless grace
Which waves in every raven tress,
  Or softly lightens o'er her face;
Where thoughts serenely sweet express
  How pure, how dear their dwelling place.

3

And on that cheek, and o'er that brow,
  So soft, so calm, yet eloquent,
The smiles that win, the tints that glow,
  But tell of days in goodness spent,
A mind at peace with all below,
  A heart whose love is innocent!

THEY SAY THAT HOPE IS HAPPINESS

Felix qui potuit rerum cognoscere causas.

Virgil

1

They say that Hope is happiness—
But genuine Love must prize the past;
And Mem'ry wakes the thoughts that bless:
They rose the first—they set the last.

2

And all that mem'ry loves the most
Was once our only hope to be:
And all that hope adored and lost
Hath melted into memory.

3

Alas! it is delusion all—
The future cheats us from afar:
Nor can we be what we recall,
Nor dare we think on what we are.

OH! SNATCHED AWAY IN BEAUTY'S BLOOM

Oh! snatched away in beauty's bloom,
On thee shall press no ponderous tomb;
    But on thy turf shall roses rear
    Their leaves, the earliest of the year;
And the wild cypress wave in tender gloom:

And oft by yon blue gushing stream
    Shall Sorrow lean her drooping head,
And feed deep thought with many a dream,
    And lingering pause and lightly tread;
    Fond wretch! as if her step disturbed the dead!

Away! we know that tears are vain,
    That death nor heeds nor hears distress:
Will this unteach us to complain?
    Or make one mourner weep the less?
And thou—who tell'st me to forget,
Thy looks are wan, thine eyes are wet.

THE VISION OF BELSHAZZAR

The King was on his throne,
  The Satraps thronged the hall:
A thousand bright lamps shone
  O'er that high festival.
A thousand cups of gold,
  In Judah deemed divine—
Jehovah's vessels hold
  The godless Heathen's wine.

In that same hour and hall,
  The fingers of a hand
Came forth against the wall,
  And wrote as if on sand:
The fingers of a man—
  A solitary hand
Along the letters ran,
  And traced them like a wand.

The monarch saw, and shook,
  And bade no more rejoice;
All bloodless waxed his look,
  And tremulous his voice.
"Let the men of lore appear,
  The wisest of the earth,
And expound the words of fear,
  Which mar our royal mirth."

Chaldea's seers are good,
  But here they have no skill;
And the unknown letters stood
  Untold and awful still.

And Babel's men of age
   Are wise and deep in lore;
But now they were not sage,
   They saw—but knew no more.

A captive in the land,
   A stranger and a youth,
He heard the king's command,
   He saw that writing's truth.
The lamps around were bright,
   The prophecy in view;
He read it on that night—
   The morrow proved it true.

"Belshazzar's grave is made.
   His kingdom passed away,
He, in the balance weighed,
   Is light and worthless clay;
The shroud, his robe of state,
   His canopy the stone;
The Mede is at his gate!
   The Persian on his throne!"

THE DESTRUCTION OF SENNACHERIB

1

The Assyrian came down like the wolf on the fold,
And his cohorts were gleaming in purple and gold;
And the sheen of their spears was like stars on the sea,
When the blue wave rolls nightly on deep Galilee.

2

Like the leaves of the forest when Summer is green,
That host with their banners at sunset were seen:
Like the leaves of the forest when Autumn hath blown,
That host on the morrow lay withered and strown.

3

For the Angel of Death spread his wings on the blast,
And breathed in the face of the foe as he pass'd;
And the eyes of the sleepers wax'd deadly and chill,
And their hearts but once heaved, and forever grew still!

4

And there lay the steed with his nostril all wide,
But through it there roll'd not the breath of his pride:
And the foam of his gasping lay white on the turf,
And cold as the spray of the rock-beating surf.

5

And there lay the rider distorted and pale,
With the dew on his brow, and the rust on his mail;
And the tents were all silent, the banners alone,
The lances unlifted, the trumpet unblown.

And the widows of Ashur are loud in their wail,
And the idols are broke in the temple of Baal;
And the might of the Gentle, unsmote by the sword,
Hath melted like snow in the glance of the Lord!

SUN OF THE SLEEPLESS!

Sun of the sleepless! melancholy star!
Whose tearful beam glows tremulously far,
That show'st the darkness thou canst not dispel,
How like art thou to joy remembered well!
So gleams the past, the light of other days,
Which shines, but warms not with its powerless rays;
A night-beam Sorrow watcheth to behold,
Distinct, but distant—clear—but, oh how cold!

FARE THEE WELL!

Alas! they had been friends in Youth;
But whispering tongues can poison truth;
And constancy lives in realms above:
And Life is thorny; and youth is vain:
And to be wroth with one we love,
Doth work like madness in the brain:

 •   •   •   •   •   •

But never either found another
To free the hollow heart from paining—
They stood aloof, the scars remaining,
Like cliffs, which had been rent asunder;
A dreary sea now flows between,
But neither heat, nor frost, nor thunder
Shall wholly do away, I ween,
The marks of that which once hath been.
Coleridge's Christabel [408-13, 419-26]

Fare thee well! and if forever—
 Still forever, fare *thee well*—
Even though unforgiving, never
 'Gainst thee shall my heart rebel—
Would that breast were bared before thee
 Where thy head so oft hath lain,
While that placid sleep came o'er thee
 Which thou ne'er can'st know again:
Would that breast by thee glanc'd over,
 Every inmost thought could show!
Then, thou wouldst at last discover
 'Twas not well to spurn it so—
Though the world for this commend thee—
 Though it smile upon the blow,
Even its praises must offend thee,

Founded on another's woe—
Though my many faults defaced me,
Could no other arm be found
Than the one which once embraced me,
To inflict a cureless wound!
Yet—oh, yet—thyself deceive not—
Love may sink by slow decay,
But by sudden wrench, believe not,
Hearts can thus be torn away;
Still thine own its life retaineth—
Still must mine—though bleeding—beat,
And the undying thought which paineth
Is—that we no more may meet—
These are words of deeper sorrow
Than the wail above the dead,
Both shall live—but every morrow
Wake us from a widowed bed—
And when thou wouldst solace gather—
When our child's first accents flow—
Wilt thou teach her to say—"Father!"
Though his care she must forgo?
When her little hands shall press thee—
When her lip to thine is pressed—
Think of him whose prayer shall bless thee—
Think of him thy love had bless'd.
Should her lineaments resemble
Those thou never more may'st see—
Then thy heart will softly tremble
With a pulse yet true to me—
All my faults—perchance thou knowest—
All my madness—none can know;
All my hopes—where'er thou goest—
Wither—yet with *thee* they go—
Every feeling hath been shaken,
Pride which not a world could bow—
Bows to thee—by thee forsaken

Even my soul forsakes me now—
But 'tis done—all words are idle—
Words from me are vainer still;
But the thoughts we cannot bridle
Force their way without the will—
Fare thee well!—thus disunited—
Torn from every nearer tie—
Seared in heart—and lone—and blighted—
More than this, I scarce can die.

STANZAS FOR MUSIC

There be none of beauty's daughters
   With a magic like thee;
And like music on the waters
   Is thy sweet voice to me:
When, as if its sound were causing
The charméd ocean's pausing,
The waves lie still and gleaming,
And the lulled winds seem dreaming:

And the midnight moon is weaving
   Her bright chain o'er the deep;
Whose breast is gently heaving,
   As an infant's asleep:
So the spirit bows before thee,
To listen and adore thee;
With a full but soft emotion,
Like the swell of summer's ocean.

A FRAGMENT

Could I remount the river of my years
To the first fountain of our smiles and tears
I would not trace again its stream of hours
Between its outworn banks of withered flowers.
But bid it flow as now—until it glides
Into the number of the nameless tides.
What is this death—a quiet of the heart—
The whole of that of which we are a part—
For life is but a vision—what I see
Of all which lives alone is life to me
And being so—the Absent are the dead
Who haunt us from tranquility—and spread
A dreary shroud around us—and invest
With sad remembrancers our hours of rest.
The absent are the dead—for they are cold,
And ne'er can be what once we did behold
And they are changed—and cheerless—or if yet
The unforgotten do not all forget—
Since thus divided—equal must it be
If the deep barrier be of earth or sea—
It may be both—but one day end it must
In the dark union of insensate dust.
The underearth inhabitants—are they
But mingled millions decomposed to clay—
The ashes of a thousand Ages spread
Wherever Man has trodden or shall tread—
Or do they in their silent cities dwell
Each in his incommunicative cell—
Or have they their own language—and a sense
Of breathless being—darkened and intense—
As midnight in her solitude—Oh Earth!

Where are the past—and wherefore had they birth?
The dead are thy inheritors—and we
But bubbles on thy surface—and the key
Of thy profundity is in the grave,
The portal of thy universal cave—
Where I would walk in Spirit—and behold
Our elements resolved to things untold,
And fathom hidden wonders—and explore
The essence of great bosoms now no more.

CHURCHILL'S GRAVE

A Fact Literally Rendered

I stood beside the grave of him who blazed
    The comet of a season, and I saw
The humblest of all sepulchers, and gazed
    With not the less of sorrow and of awe
On that neglected turf and quiet stone,
With name no clearer than the names unknown,
Which lay unread around it; and I asked
    The Gardener of that ground, why it might be
That for this plant strangers his memory tasked,
    Through the thick deaths of half a century?
And thus he answered—"Well, I do not know
Why frequent travelers turn to pilgrims so;
He died before my day of Sextonship,
    And I had not the digging of this grave."
And is this all? I thought—and do we rip
    The veil of Immortality, and crave
I know not what of honor and of light
Through unborn ages, to endure this blight,
So soon, and so successless? As I said,
The Architect of all on which we tread,
For Earth is but a tombstone, did essay
To extricate remembrance from the clay,
Whose minglings might confuse a Newton's thought
    Were it not that all life must end in one,
Of which we are but dreamers—as he caught
    As 'twere the twilight of a former Sun,
Thus spoke he—"I believe the man of whom
You wot, who lies in this selected tomb,
Was a most famous writer in his day,
And therefore travelers step from out their way

To pay him honor—and myself whate'er
    Your honor pleases"—then most pleased I shook
    From out my pocket's avaricious nook
Some certain coins of silver, which as 'twere
Perforce I gave this man, though I could spare
So much but inconveniently—Ye smile,
I see ye, ye profane ones! all the while,
Because my homely phrase the truth would tell.
You are the fools, not I—for I did dwell
With a deep thought, and with a softened eye,
On that Old Sexton's natural homily,
In which there was Obscurity and Fame—
The Glory and the Nothing of a Name.

STANZAS TO AUGUSTA

1

Though the day of my destiny's over,
  And the star of my fate hath declined,
Thy soft heart refused to discover
  The faults which so many could find;
Though thy soul with my grief was acquainted,
  It shrunk not to share it with me,
And the love which my spirit hath painted
  It never hath found but in *thee*.

2

Then when nature around me is smiling
  The last smile which answers to mine,
I do not believe it beguiling
  Because it reminds me of thine;
And when winds are at war with the ocean,
  As the breasts I believed in with me,
If their billows excite an emotion
  It is that they bear me from *thee*.

3

Though the rock of my last hope is shiver'd,
  And its fragments are sunk in the wave,
Though I feel that my soul is deliver'd
  To pain—it shall not be its slave.
There is many a pang to pursue me:
  They may crush, but they shall not contemn—
They may torture, but shall not subdue me—
  'Tis of *thee* that I think—not of them.

4

Thou human, thou didst not deceive me,
  Though woman, thou didst not forsake,
Though loved, thou foreborest to grieve me,
  Though slander'd, thou never could'st shake—
Though trusted, thou didst not betray me,
  Though parted, it was not to fly,
Though watchful, 'twas not to defame me,
  Nor, mute, that the world might belie.

5

Yet I blame not the world, nor despise it,
  Nor the war of the many with one—
If my soul was not fitted to prize it
  'Twas folly not sooner to shun:
And if dearly that error hath cost me,
  And more than I once could foresee,
I have found that, whatever it lost me,
  It could not deprive me of *thee*.

6

From the wreck of my past, which hath perish'd,
  Thus much I at least may recall,
It hath taught me that what I most cherish'd
  Deserved to be dearest of all:
In the desert a fountain is springing,
  In the wide waste there still is a tree,
And a bird in the solitude singing,
  Which speaks to my spirit of *thee*.

EPISTLE TO AUGUSTA

1

My Sister—my sweet Sister—if a name
   Dearer and purer were—it should be thine.
Mountains and Seas divide us—but I claim
   No tears—but tenderness to answer mine:
Go where I will, to me thou art the same—
   A loved regret which I would not resign—
There yet are two things in my destiny
A world to roam through—and a home with thee.

2

The first were nothing—had I still the last
   It were the haven of my happiness—
But other claims and other ties thou hast—
   And mine is not the wish to make them less.
A strange doom was thy father's son's and past
   Recalling—as it lies beyond redress—
Reversed for him our grandsire's fate of yore
He had no rest at sea—nor I on shore.

3

If my inheritance of storms hath been
   In other elements—and on the rocks
Of perils overlooked or unforeseen
   I have sustained my share of worldly shocks
The fault was mine—nor do I seek to screen
   My errors with defensive paradox—
I have been cunning in mine overthrow
The careful pilot of my proper woe.

4

Mine were my faults—and mine be their reward—
  My whole life was a contest—since the day
That gave me being gave me that which marred
  The gift—a fate or will that walked astray—
And I at times have found the struggle hard
  And thought of shaking off my bonds of clay—
But now I fain would for a time survive
If but to see what next can well arrive.

5

Kingdoms and empires in my little day
  I have outlived and yet I am not old—
And when I look on this, the petty spray
  Of my own years of trouble, which have rolled
Like a wild bay of breakers, melts away—
  Something—l know no what—does still uphold
A spirit of slight patience—not in vain
Even for its own sake do we purchase pain.

6

Perhaps—the workings of defiance stir
  Within me—or perhaps a cold despair—
Brought on when ills habitually recur—
  Perhaps a harder clime—or purer air—
For to all such may change of soul refer—
  And with light armor we may learn to bear—
Have taught me a strange quiet—which was not
The chief companion of a calmer lot.

7

I feel almost at times as I have felt
  In happy childhood—trees and flowers and brooks
Which do remember me of where I dwelt

Ere my young mind was sacrificed to books—
Come as of yore upon me—and can melt
My heart with recognition of their looks—
And even at moments I could think I see
Some living things to love—but none like thee.

8

Here are the Alpine landscapes—which create
A fund for contemplation—to admire
Is a brief feeling of a trivial date—
But something worthier do such scenes inspire:
Here to be lonely is not desolate—
For much I view which I could most desire—
And above all a lake I can behold—
Lovelier—not dearer—than our own of old.

9

Oh that thou wert but with me!—but I grow
The fool of my own wishes—and forget
The solitude which I have vaunted so
Has lost its praise in this but one regret—
There may be others which I less may show—
I am not of the plaintive mood—and yet
I feel an ebb in my philosophy
And the tide rising in my altered eye.

10

I did remind thee of our own dear lake
By the old Hall which may be mine no more—
Leman's is fair—but think not I forsake
The sweet remembrance of a dearer shore—
Sad havoc Time must with my memory make
Ere *that* or *thou* can fade these eyes before—
Though like all things which I have loved—they are
Resigned forever—or divided far.

11

The world is all before me—I but ask
    Of Nature that with which she will comply—
It is but in her Summer's sun to bask—
    To mingle in the quiet of her sky—
To see her gentle face without a mask
    And never gaze on it with apathy—
She was my early friend—and now shall be
My Sister—till I look again on thee.

12

I can reduce all feelings but this one
    And that I would not—for at length I see
Such scenes as those wherein my life begun
    The earliest—were the only paths for me.
Had I but sooner known the crowd to shun
    I had been better than I now can be
The passions which have torn me would have slept—
I had not suffered—and *thou* hadst not wept.

13

With false Ambition what had I to do?
    Little with love, and least of all with fame!
And yet they came unsought and with me grew,
    And made me all which they can make—a Name.
Yet this was not the end I did pursue—
    Surely I once beheld a nobler aim.
But all is over—I am one the more
To baffled millions which have gone before.

14

And for the future—this world's future may
    From me demand but little from my care;
I have outlived myself by many a day,

Having survived so many things that were—
My years have been no slumber—but the prey
    Of ceaseless vigils—for I had the share
Of life which might have filled a century
Before its fourth in time had passed me by.

15

And for the remnants which may be to come
    I am content—and for the past I feel
Not thankless—for within the crowded sum
    Of struggles—happiness at times would steal—
And for the present—I would not benumb
    My feelings farther—nor shall I conceal
That with all this I still can look around
And worship Nature with a thought profound.

16

For thee—my own sweet Sister—in thy heart
    I know myself secure—as thou in mine
We were and are—I am—even as thou art—
    Beings—who ne'er each other can resign
It is the same together or apart—
    From life's commencement to its slow decline—
We are entwined—let death come slow or fast—
The tie which bound the first endures the last.

DARKNESS

I had a dream, which was not all a dream.
The bright sun was extinguish'd, and the stars
Did wander darkling in the eternal space,
Rayless, and pathless, and the icy earth
Swung blind and blackening in the moonless air;
Morn came, and went—and came, and brought no day,
And men forgot their passions in the dread
Of this their desolation; and all hearts
Were chill'd into a selfish prayer for light:
And they did live by watchfires—and the thrones,
The palaces of crowned kings—the huts,
The habitations of all things which dwell,
Were burnt for beacons; cities were consumed,
And men were gathered round their blazing homes
To look once more into each other's face;
Happy were those who dwelt within the eye
Of the volcanoes, and their mountain torch:
A fearful hope was all the world contain'd;
Forests were set on fire—but hour by hour
They fell and faded—and the crackling trunks
Extinguish'd with a crash—and all was black.
The brows of men by the despairing light
Wore an unearthly aspect, as by fits
The flashes fell upon them; some lay down
And hid their eyes and wept; and some did rest
Their chins upon their clenched hands, and smiled;
And others hurried to and fro, and fed
Their funeral piles with fuel, and looked up
With mad disquietude on the dull sky,
The pall of a past world; and then again
With curses cast them down upon the dust,

And gnash'd their teeth and howl'd: the wild birds shriek'd,
And, terrified, did flutter on the ground,
And flap their useless wings; the wildest brutes
Came tame and tremulous; and vipers crawl'd
And twined themselves among the multitude,
Hissing, but stingless—they were slain for food:
And War, which for a moment was no more,
Did glut himself again—a meal was bought
With blood, and each sate sullenly apart
Gorging himself in gloom: no love was left;
All earth was but one thought—and that was death,
Immediate and inglorious; and the pang
Of famine fed upon all entrails—men
Died, and their bones were tombless as their flesh;
The meager by the meager were devoured,
Even dogs assail'd their masters, all save one,
And he was faithful to a corse, and kept
The birds and beasts and famish'd men at bay,
Till hunger clung them, or the dropping dead
Lured their lank jaws; himself sought out no food,
But with a piteous and perpetual moan
And a quick desolate cry, licking the hand
Which answered not with a caress—he died.
The crowd was famish'd by degrees; but two
Of an enormous city did survive,
And they were enemies; they met beside
The dying embers of an altar place
Where had been heap'd a mass of holy things
For an unholy usage; they raked up,
And shivering scraped with their cold skeleton hands
The feeble ashes, and their feeble breath
Blew for a little life, and made a flame
Which was a mockery; then they lifted up
Their eyes as it grew lighter, and beheld
Each other's aspects—saw, and shriek'd, and died—
Even of their mutual hideousness they died,

Unknowing who he was upon whose brow
Famine had written Fiend. The world was void,
The populous and the powerful—was a lump,
Seasonless, herbless, treeless, manless, lifeless—
A lump of death—a chaos of hard clay.
The rivers, lakes, and ocean all stood still,
And nothing stirred within their silent depths;
Ships sailorless lay rotting on the sea,
And their masts fell down piecemeal; as they dropp'd
They slept on the abyss without a surge—
The waves were dead; the tides were in their grave,
The moon their mistress had expired before;
The winds were withered in the stagnant air,
And the clouds perish'd; Darkness had no need
Of aid from them—She was the universe.

PROMETHEUS

1

Titan! To whose immortal eyes
  The sufferings of mortality,
  Seen in their sad reality,
Were not as things that gods despise;
What was thy pity's recompense?
A silent suffering, and intense;
The rock, the vulture, and the chain,
All that the proud can feel of pain,
The agony they do not show,
The suffocating sense of woe,
  Which speaks but in its loneliness,
And then is jealous lest the sky
Should have a listener, nor will sigh
  Until its voice is echoless.

2

Titan! to thee the strife was given
  Between the suffering and the will,
  Which torture where they cannot kill;
And the inexorable Heaven,
And the deaf tyranny of Fate,
The ruling principle of Hate,
Which for its pleasure doth create
The things it may annihilate,
Refused thee even the boon to die:
The wretched gift eternity
Was thine—and thou hast borne it well.
All that the Thunderer wrung from thee
Was but the menace which flung back

On him the torments of thy rack;
The fate thou didst so well foresee
But would not to appease him tell;
And in thy Silence was his Sentence,
And in his Soul a vain repentance,
And evil dread so ill dissembled
That in his hand the lightnings trembled.

3

Thy Godlike crime was to be kind,
To render with thy precepts less
The sum of human wretchedness,
And strengthen Man with his own mind;
But baffled as thou wert from high,
Still in thy patient energy,
In the endurance, and repulse
Of thine impenetrable Spirit,
Which Earth and Heaven could not convulse,
A mighty lesson we inherit:
Thou art a symbol and a sign
To Mortals of their fate and force;
Like thee, Man is in part divine,
A troubled stream from a pure source;
And Man in portions can foresee
His own funereal destiny;
His wretchedness, and his resistance,
And his sad unallied existence:
To which his Spirit may oppose
Itself—an equal to all woes,
And a firm will, and a deep sense,
Which even in torture can descry
Its own concentered recompense,
Triumphant where it dares defy,
And making Death a Victory.

SONNET ON CHILLON

Eternal Spirit of the chainless Mind!
   Brightest in dungeons, Liberty! thou art;
   For there thy habitation is the heart—
The heart which love of thee alone can bind;
And when thy sons to fetters are consigned—
   To fetters, and the damp vault's dayless gloom,
   Their country conquers with their martyrdom,
And Freedom's fame finds wings on every wind.
Chillon! thy prison is a holy place,
   And thy sad floor an altar—for 'twas trod,
Until his very steps have left a trace
   Worn, as if thy cold pavement were a sod,
By Bonnivard!—May none those marks efface!
   For they appeal from tyranny to God.

SONNET TO LAKE LEMAN

Rousseau—Voltaire—our Gibbon—and De Staël—
   Leman! these names are worthy of thy shore,
   Thy shore of names like these! wert thou no more,
Their memory thy remembrance would recall:
To them thy banks were lovely as to all,
   But they have made them lovelier, for the lore
   Of mighty minds doth hallow in the core
Of human hearts the ruin of a wall
   Where dwelt the wise and wondrous; but by *thee*,
How much more, Lake of Beauty! do we feel,
   In sweetly gliding o'er thy crystal sea,
The wild glow of that not ungentle zeal,
   Which of the heirs of immortality
Is proud, and makes the breath of glory real!

SO, WE'LL GO NO MORE A-ROVING

1

So, we'll go no more a-roving
So late into the night,
Though the heart be still as loving,
And the moon be still as bright.

2

For the sword outwears its sheath,
And the soul wears out the breast,
And the heart must pause to breathe,
And love itself have rest.

3

Though the night was made for loving,
And the day returns too soon,
Yet we'll go no more a-roving
By the light of the moon.

TO THOMAS MOORE

My boat is on the shore,
  And my bark is on the sea;
But, before I go, Tom Moore,
  Here's a double health to thee!

Here's a sigh to those who love me,
  And a smile to those who hate;
And, whatever sky's above me,
  Here's a heart for every fate.

Though the ocean roar around me,
  Yet it still shall bear me on;
Though a desert should surround me,
  It hath springs that may be won.

Were't the last drop in the well,
  As I gasped upon the brink,
Ere my fainting spirit fell,
  'Tis to thee that I would drink.

With that water, as this wine,
  The libation I would pour
Should be—peace with thine and mine,
  And a health to thee, Tom Moore.

STANZAS

1

Could Love forever
Run like a river
And Time's Endeavor
   Be tried in vain,
No other Pleasure
With this could measure
And like a Treasure
   We'd hug the chain.
But since our sighing
Ends not in dying
And formed for flying
   Love plumes his wing,
Then for this reason
Let's love a Season,
But let that Season be only *Spring*—

2

When lovers parted
Feel brokenhearted,
And all hopes thwarted
   Expect to die,
A few years older
Ah! how much colder
They might behold her
   For whom they sigh;
When linked together
Through every weather
We pluck Love's feather
   From out his wing;

He'll sadly shiver
And droop forever
Without the plumage that sped his Spring—

3

Like Chiefs of Faction
His Life is Action,
A formal paction,
    Which curbs his reign,
Obscures his Glory,
Despot no more, he
Such Territory
    Quits with disdain.
Still—still—advancing
With banners glancing
His power enhancing
    He must march on;
Repose but cloys him,
Retreat destroys him,
Love brooks not a degraded throne!

4

Wait not, fond Lover!
Till years are over,
And then recover
    As from a dream.
While each bewailing
The other's failing
With wrath and railing
    All hideous seem;
While first decreasing
Yet not quite ceasing,
Pause not—till teasing
    All passion blight;
If once diminished

His reign is finished,
One last embrace then, and bid Good Night!

5

So shall Affection
To recollection
The dear connection
    Bring back with joy,
You have not waited
Till tired and hated
All passions sated
    Began to cloy.
Your last embraces
Leave no cold traces,
The same fond faces
    As through the past,
And Eyes the Mirrors
Of your sweet Errors
Reflect but Rapture not least though last.

6

True! Separations
Ask more than patience—
What desperations
    From such have risen!
And yet remaining,
What is't but chaining
Hearts, which once waning
    Beat 'gainst their prison;
Time can but cloy Love,
And Use destroy Love,
The winged Boy Love
    Is but for boys.
You'll find it torture
Though sharper, shorter,
To wean and not wear out your Joys.

TO THE PO. JUNE 2, 1819

River! that rollest by the ancient walls
  Where dwells the Lady of my Love, when she
Walks by thy brink and there perchance recalls
  A faint and fleeting memory of me,
What if thy deep and ample stream should be
  A mirror of my heart, where she may read
The thousand thoughts I now betray to thee
  Wild as thy wave and headlong as thy speed?
What do I say? "a mirror of my heart"?
  Are not thy waters sweeping, dark, and strong,
Such as my feelings were and are, thou art,
  And such as thou art were my passions long.
Time may have somewhat tamed them, not forever
  Thou overflow'st thy banks, and not for aye
The bosom overboils, congenial River!
  Thy floods subside, and mine have sunk away,
But left long wrecks behind us, yet again
  Borne on our old career unchanged we move,
Thou tendest wildly to the wilder main
  And I to loving one I should not love.
The current I behold will sweep beneath
  Her palace walls, and murmur at her feet,
Her eyes will look on thee, when she shall breathe
  The twilight air unchained from Summer's heat.
She will look on thee—I have looked on thee
  Full of that thought, and from this moment ne'er
Thy waters could I name, hear named, or see
  Without the inseparable Sigh for her.
Her bright eyes will be imaged in thy Stream—
  Yes, they will meet the wave I gaze on now,
But mine can not even witness in a dream

That happy wave repass me in its flow.
The wave that bears my tears returns no more
    Will She return by whom that wave shall sweep?
Both tread thy bank, both wander by thy shore,
    I near thy source, and She by the blue deep.
But that which keepeth us apart, is not
    Distance, nor depth of wave, nor space of earth,
But the distractions of a various lot,
    Ah! various as the climates of our birth!
A Stranger loves a lady of the land,
    Born far beyond the Mountains, but his blood
Is all meridian, as if never fanned
    By the bleak wind that chills the Polar flood.
My heart is all meridian, were it not
    I had not suffered now, nor should I be—
Despite of tortures ne'er to be forgot
    The Slave again, Oh Love! at least of thee!
'Tis vain to struggle, I have struggled long
    To love again no more as once I loved.
Oh! Time! why leave this earliest Passion strong?
    To tear a heart which pants to be unmoved?

STANZAS

When a man hath no freedom to fight for at home,
  Let him combat for that of his neighbors;
Let him think of the glories of Greece and of Rome,
  And get knock'd on the head for his labors.

To do good to mankind is the chivalrous plan,
  And is always as nobly requited;
Then battle for freedom wherever you can,
  And, if not shot or hang'd, you'll get knighted.

JOHN KEATS

Who killed John Keats?
  "I," says the Quarterly,
So savage and Tartarly;
  "'Twas one of my feats."

Who shot the arrow?
  "The poet-priest Milman
(So ready to kill man),
  Or Southey or Barrow."

STANZAS

WRITTEN ON THE ROAD BETWEEN FLORENCE AND PISA

Oh, talk not to me of a name great in story;
The days of your youth are the days of our glory;
And the myrtle and ivy of sweet two-and-twenty
Are worth all your laurels, though ever so plenty.

What are garlands and crowns to the brow that is
    wrinkled?
'Tis but as a dead flower with May-dew besprinkled.
Then away with all such from the head that is hoary!
What care I for the wreaths that can *only* give glory?

Oh Fame!—if I e'er took delight in thy praises,
'Twas less for the sake of thy high-sounding phrases,
Than to see the bright eyes of the dear one discover
She thought that I was not unworthy to love her.

There chiefly I sought thee, *there* only I found thee;
Her glance was the best of the rays that surround thee;
When it sparkled o'er aught that was bright in my story,
I knew it was love, and I felt it was glory.

ON THIS DAY I COMPLETE MY THIRTY-SIXTH YEAR

MESSALONGHI. JANUARY 22, 1824.

'Tis time this heart should be unmoved,
　　Since others it hath ceased to move:
Yet though I cannot be beloved,
　　　　Still let me love!

My days are in the yellow leaf;
　　The flowers and fruits of Love are gone;
The worm—the canker, and the grief
　　　　Are mine alone!

The fire that on my bosom preys
　　Is lone as some Volcanic Isle;
No torch is kindled at its blaze
　　　　A funeral pile!

The hope, the fear, the jealous care,
　　The exalted portion of the pain
And power of Love I cannot share,
　　　　But wear the chain.

But 'tis not *thus*—and 'tis not *here*
　　Such thoughts should shake my Soul, nor *now*
Where Glory decks the hero's bier
　　　　Or binds his brow.

The Sword, the Banner, and the Field,
　　Glory and Greece around us see!
The Spartan borne upon his shield
　　　　Was not more free!

Awake (not Greece—she *is* awake!)
  Awake, my Spirit! think through whom
Thy life-blood tracks its parent lake
      And then strike home!

Tread those reviving passions down
Unworthy Manhood—unto thee
Indifferent should the smile or frown
      Of Beauty be.

If thou regret'st thy Youth, *why live?*
  The land of honorable Death
Is here—up to the Field, and give
      Away thy Breath!

Seek out—less often sought than found—
A Soldier's Grave, for thee the best;
Then look around, and choose thy Ground,
      And take thy Rest!

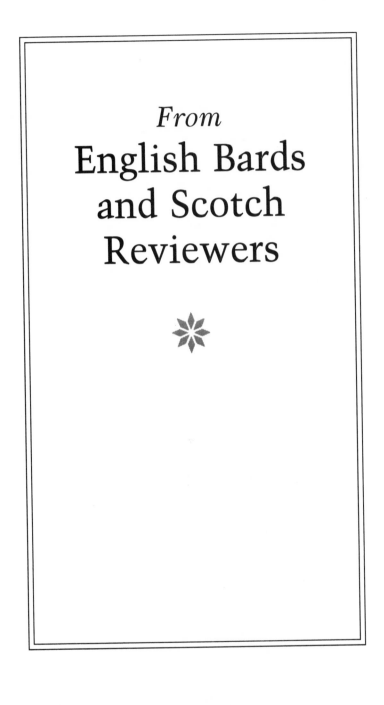

From

English Bards
and Scotch
Reviewers

From

ENGLISH BARDS AND SCOTCH REVIEWERS

A Satire

I had rather be a kitten, and cry, mew!
Than one of these same meter ballad-mongers,
    Shakespeare [*1 Henry IV*, III. i. 128-9].

Such shameless Bards we have; and yet 'tis true,
There are as mad, abandon'd Critics too.
    Pope [*Essay on Criticism*, 610-11].

    Time was, ere yet in these degenerate days
Ignoble themes obtained mistaken praise,
When Sense and Wit with Poesy allied,
No fabled Graces, flourished side by side,
From the same fount their inspiration drew,
And, reared by Taste, bloomed fairer as they grew.
Then, in this happy Isle, a POPE's pure strain
Sought the rapt soul to charm, nor sought in vain;
A polished nation's praise aspired to claim,
And rais'd the people's, as the poet's fame.
Like him great DRYDEN poured the tide of song,
In stream less smooth indeed, yet doubly strong.
Then CONGREVE's scenes could cheer, or OTWAY's
    melt;
For Nature then an English audience felt—
But why these names, or greater still, retrace,
When all to feebler Bards resign their place?
Yet to such times our lingering looks are cast,
When taste and reason with those times are past.
Now look around, and turn each trifling page,

Survey the precious works that please the age;
This truth at least let Satire's self allow,
No dearth of Bards can be complained of now:
The loaded Press beneath her labor groans,
And Printer's devils shake their weary bones,
While SOUTHEY's Epics cram the creaking shelves,
And LITTLE's Lyrics shine in hot-pressed twelves.

Thus saith the Preacher; "nought beneath the sun
Is new," yet still from change to change we run.
What varied wonders tempt us as they pass!
The Cow-pox, Tractors, Galvanism, and Gas
In turns appear to make the vulgar stare,
Till the swoln bubble bursts—and all is air!
Nor less new schools of poetry arise,
Where dull pretenders grapple for the prize:
O'er Taste awhile these Pseudo-bards prevail;
Each country Book-club bows the knee to Baal,
And, hurling lawful Genius from the throne,
Erects a shrine and idol of its own;
Some leaden calf—but whom it matters not,
From soaring SOUTHEY, down to groveling STOTT.

Behold! in various throngs the scribbling crew,
For notice eager, pass in long review:
Each spurs his jaded Pegasus apace,
And Rhyme and Blank maintain an equal race;
Sonnets on sonnets crowd, and ode on ode;
And Tales of Terror jostle on the road;
Immeasurable measures move along,
For simpering Folly loves a varied song,
To strange, mysterious Dullness still the friend,
Admires the strain she cannot comprehend.
Thus Lays of Minstrels—may they be the last!—
On half-strung harps, whine mournful to the blast,
While mountain spirits prate to river sprites,

That dames may listen to the sound at nights;
And goblin brats of Gilpin Horner's brood
Decoy young Border-nobles through the wood,
And skip at every step, Lord knows how high,
And frighten foolish babes, the Lord knows why,
While highborn ladies, in their magic cell,
Forbidding Knights to read who cannot spell,
Dispatch a courier to a wizard's grave,
And fight with honest men to shield a knave.

Next view in state, proud prancing on his roan,
The golden-crested haughty Marmion,
Now forging scrolls, now foremost in the fight,
Not quite a Felon, yet but half a Knight,
The gibbet or the field prepared to grace;
A mighty mixture of the great and base.
And think'st thou, SCOTT! by vain conceit perchance,
On public taste to foist thy stale romance,
Though MURRAY with his MILLER may combine
To yield thy muse just half-a-crown per line?
No! when the sons of song descend to trade,
Their bays are sear, their former laurels fade.
Let such forgo the poet's sacred name,
Who rack their brains for lucre, not for fame:
Still for stern Mammon may they toil in vain!
And sadly gaze on Gold they cannot gain!
Such be their meed, such still the just reward
Of prostituted Muse, and hireling Bard!
For this we spurn Apollo's venal son,
And bid a long, "good night to Marmion."

These are the themes, that claim our plaudits now;
These are the Bards to whom the Muse must bow;
While MILTON, DRYDEN, POPE, alike forgot,
Resign their hallow'd Bays to WALTER SCOTT.

The time has been, when yet the Muse was young,
When HOMER swept the lyre, and MARO sung,
An Epic scarce ten centuries could claim,
While awestruck nations hailed the magic name:
The work of each immortal Bard appears
The single wonder of a thousand years.
Empires have moldered from the face of earth,
Tongues have expired with those who gave them birth,
Without the glory such a strain can give,
As even in ruin bids the language live.
Not so with us, though minor Bards content,
On one great work a life of labor spent:
With eagle pinion soaring to the skies,
Behold the Ballad-monger SOUTHEY rise!
To him let CAMOENS, MILTON, TASSO, yield,
Whose annual strains, like armies, take the field.
First in the ranks see Joan of Arc advance,
The scourge of England, and the boast of France!
Though burnt by wicked BEDFORD for a witch,
Behold her statue placed in Glory's niche;
Her fetters burst, and just released from prison,
A virgin Phoenix from her ashes risen.
Next see tremendous Thalaba come on,
Arabia's monstrous, wild, and wond'rous son;
Domdaniel's dread destroyer, who o'erthrew
More mad magicians than the world e'er knew.
Immortal Hero! all thy foes o'ercome,
Forever reign—the rival of Tom Thumb!
Since startled Meter fled before thy face,
Well wert thou doomed the last of all thy race!
Well might triumphant Genii bear thee hence,
Illustrious conqueror of common sense!
Now, last and greatest, Madoc spreads his sails,
Cacique in Mexico, and Prince in Wales:
Tells us strange tales, as other travelers do,
More old than Mandeville's, and not so true.

Oh! SOUTHEY, SOUTHEY! cease thy varied song!
A Bard may chaunt too often, and too long:
As thou art strong in verse, in mercy spare!
A fourth, alas! were more than we could bear.
But if, in spite of all the world can say,
Thou still wilt verseward plod thy weary way;
If still in Berkeley-Ballads most uncivil,
Thou wilt devote old women to the devil,
The babe unborn thy dread intent may rue:
"God help thee," SOUTHEY, and thy readers too.

Next comes the dull disciple of thy school,
That mild apostate from poetic rule,
The simple WORDSWORTH, framer of a lay
As soft as evening in his favorite May;
Who warns his friend "to shake off toil and trouble,
And quit his books, for fear of growing double";
Who, both by precept and example, shows
That prose is verse, and verse is merely prose,
Convincing all by demonstration plain,
Poetic souls delight in prose insane;
And Christmas stories tortured into rhyme,
Contain the essence of the true sublime:
Thus when he tells the tale of Betty Foy,
The idiot mother of "an idiot Boy";
A moonstruck silly lad who lost his way,
And, like his Bard, confounded night with day,
So close on each pathetic part he dwells,
And each adventure so sublimely tells,
That all who view the "idiot in his glory,"
Conceive the Bard the hero of the story.

Shall gentle COLERIDGE pass unnoticed here,
To turgid ode, and tumid stanza dear?
Though themes of innocence amuse him best,
Yet still obscurity's a welcome guest.

If inspiration should her aid refuse,
To him who takes a Pixy for a Muse,
Yet none in lofty numbers can surpass
The Bard who soars to elegize an ass:
So well the subject suits his noble mind,
He brays the Laureat of the long-ear'd kind!

From

Childe Harold's
Pilgrimage

A ROMAUNT

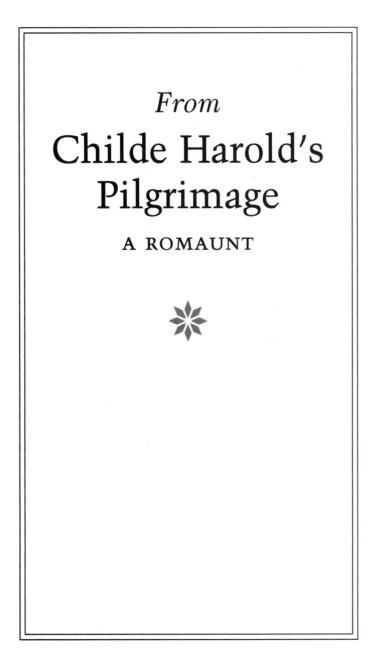

From CANTO I

1

Oh, thou! in Hellas deem'd of heav'nly birth,
Muse! form'd or fabled at the minstrel's will!
Since sham'd full oft by later lyres on earth,
Mine dares not call thee from thy sacred hill:
Yet there I've wander'd by thy vaunted rill;
Yes! sigh'd o'er Delphi's long-deserted shrine,
Where, save that feeble fountain, all is still;
Nor mote my shell awake the weary Nine
To grace so plain a tale—this lowly lay of mine.

2

Whilome in Albion's isle there dwelt a youth,
Who ne in virtue's ways did take delight;
But spent his days in riot most uncouth,
And vex'd with mirth the drowsy ear of Night.
Ah, me! in sooth he was a shameless wight,
Sore given to revel and ungodly glee;
Few earthly things found favor in his sight
Save concubines and carnal company,
And flaunting wassailers of high and low degree.

3

Childe Harold was he hight—but whence his name
And lineage long, it suits me not to say;
Suffice it, that perchance they were of fame,
And had been glorious in another day:
But one sad losel soils a name for aye,
However mighty in the olden time;
Nor all that heralds rake from coffin'd clay,
Nor florid prose, nor honied lies of rhyme
Can blazon evil deeds, or consecrate a crime.

4

Childe Harold bask'd him in the noontide sun,
Disporting there like any other fly;
Nor deem'd before his little day was done
One blast might chill him into misery.
But long ere scarce a third of his pass'd by,
Worse than adversity the Childe befell;
He felt the fullness of satiety:
Then loath'd he in his native land to dwell,
Which seem'd to him more lone than Eremite's sad cell.

5

For he through Sin's long labyrinth had run,
Nor made atonement when he did amiss,
Had sigh'd to many though he lov'd but one,
And that lov'd one, alas! could ne'er be his.
Ah, happy she! to 'scape from him whose kiss
Had been pollution unto aught so chaste;
Who soon had left her charms for vulgar bliss,
And spoil'd her goodly lands to gild his waste,
Nor calm domestic peace had ever deign'd to taste.

6

And now Childe Harold was sore sick at heart,
And from his fellow bacchanals would flee;
'Tis said, at times the sullen tear would start,
But Pride congeal'd the drop within his ee:
Apart he stalk'd in joyless reverie,
And from his native land resolv'd to go,
And visit scorching climes beyond the sea;
With pleasure drugg'd he almost long'd for woe,
And e'en for change of scene would seek the shades below.

7

The Childe departed from his father's hall:
It was a vast and venerable pile;

So old, it seemed only not to fall,
Yet strength was pillar'd in each massy aisle.
Monastic dome! condemn'd to uses vile!
Where Superstition once had made her den
Now Paphian girls were known to sing and smile;
And monks might deem their time was come agen,
If ancient tales say true, nor wrong these holy men.

8

Yet oft-times in his maddest mirthful mood
Strange pangs would flash along Childe Harold's brow,
As if the memory of some deadly feud
Or disappointed passion lurk'd below:
But this none knew, nor haply car'd to know;
For his was not that open, artless soul
That feels relief by bidding sorrow flow,
Nor sought he friend to counsel or condole,
Whate'er his grief mote be, which he could not control.

9

And none did love him—though to hall and bower
He gather'd revelers from far and near,
He knew them flatt'rers of the festal hour;
The heartless parasites of present cheer.
Yea! none did love him—not his lemans dear—
But pomp and power alone are woman's care,
And where these are light Eros finds a feere;
Maidens, like moths, are ever caught by glare,
And Mammon wins his way where Seraphs might despair.

10

Childe Harold had a mother—not forgot,
Though parting from that mother he did shun;
A sister whom he lov'd, but saw her not

Before his weary pilgrimage begun:
If friends he had, he bade adieu to none.
Yet deem not thence his breast a breast of steel;
Ye, who have known what 'tis to dote upon
A few dear objects, will in sadness feel
Such partings break the heart they fondly hope to heal.

11

His house, his home, his heritage, his lands,
The laughing dames in whom he did delight,
Whose large blue eyes, fair locks, and snowy hands
Might shake the saintship of an anchorite,
And long had fed his youthful appetite;
His goblets brimm'd with every costly wine,
And all that mote to luxury invite,
Without a sigh he left, to cross the brine,
And traverse Paynim shores, and pass Earth's central line.

12

The sails were fill'd, and fair the light winds blew,
As glad to waft him from his native home;
And fast the white rocks faded from his view,
And soon were lost in circumambient foam:
And then, it may be, of his wish to roam
Repented he, but in his bosom slept
The silent thought, nor from his lips did come
One word of wail, whilst others sate and wept,
And to the reckless gales unmanly moaning kept.

13

But when the sun was sinking in the sea
He seiz'd his harp, which he at times could string,
And strike, albeit with untaught melody,
When deem'd he no strange ear was listening:
And now his fingers o'er it he did fling,

And tun'd his farewell in the dim twilight.
White flew the vessel on her snowy wing,
And fleeting shores receded from his sight,
Thus to the elements he pour'd his last "Good night."

"Adieu, adieu! my native shore
    Fades o'er the waters blue;
The Night-winds sigh, the breakers roar,
    And shrieks the wild seamew.
Yon Sun that sets upon the sea
    We follow in his flight;
Farewell awhile to him and thee,
    My native Land—Good Night.

"A few short hours and He will rise
    To give the Morrow birth;
And I shall hail the main and skies,
    But not my mother Earth.
Deserted is my own good hall,
    Its hearth is desolate;
Wild weeds are gathering on the wall;
    My dog howls at the gate.

"Come hither, hither, my little page!
    Why dost thou weep and wail?
Or dost thou dread the billows' rage,
    Or tremble at the gale?
But dash the teardrop from thine eye;
    Our ship is swift and strong:
Our fleetest falcon scarce can fly
    More merrily along."

"Let winds be shrill, let waves roll high,
    I fear not wave nor wind;
Yet marvel not, Sir Childe, that I
    Am sorrowful in mind;
For I have from my father gone,

A mother whom I love,
And have no friend, save these alone,
But thee—and one above.

"My father bless'd me fervently,
    Yet did not much complain;
But sorely will my mother sigh
    Till I come back again."—
"Enough, enough, my little lad!
    Such tears become thine eye;
If I thy guileless bosom had
    Mine own would not be dry.

"Come hither, hither, my staunch yeoman,
    Why dost thou look so pale?
Or dost thou dread a French foeman?
    Or shiver at the gale?"—
"Deem'st thou I tremble for my life?
    Sir Childe, I'm not so weak;
But thinking on an absent wife
    Will blanch a faithful cheek.

"My spouse and boys dwell near thy hall,
    Along the bordering lake,
And when they on their father call,
    What answer shall she make?"—
"Enough, enough, my yeoman good,
    Thy grief let none gainsay;
But I, who am of lighter mood,
    Will laugh to flee away.

"For who would trust the seeming sighs
    Of wife or paramour?
Fresh feres will dry the bright blue eyes
    We late saw streaming o'er.
For Pleasures past I do not grieve,

Nor perils gathering near;
  My greatest grief is that I leave
    No thing that claims a tear.

"And now I'm in the world alone,
    Upon the wide, wide sea:
But why should I for others groan,
    When none will sigh for me?
Perchance my dog will whine in vain,
    Till fed by stranger hands;
But long ere I come back again,
    He'd tear me where he stands.

"With thee, my bark, I'll swiftly go
    Athwart the foaming brine;
Nor care what land thou bear'st me to,
    So not again to mine.
Welcome, welcome, ye dark-blue waves!
    And when you fail my sight,
Welcome, ye deserts, and ye caves!
    My native Land—Good Night."

From CANTO II

1

Come, blue-eyed maid of heaven!—but thou, alas!
Didst never yet one mortal song inspire—
Goddess of Wisdom! here thy temple was,
And is, despite of war and wasting fire,
And years, that bade thy worship to expire:
But worse than steel, and flame, and ages slow,
Is the dread scepter and dominion dire
Of men who never felt the sacred glow.
That thoughts of thee and thine on polish'd breasts bestow.

2

Ancient of days! august Athena! where,
Where are thy men of might? thy grand in soul?
Gone—glimmering through the dream of things that were:
First in the race that led to Glory's goal,
They won, and pass'd away—is this the whole?
A schoolboy's tale, the wonder of an hour!
The warrior's weapon and the sophist's stole
Are sought in vain, and o'er each moldering tower,
Dim with the mist of years, gray flits the shade of power.

3

Son of the morning, rise! approach you here!
Come—but molest not yon defenseless urn:
Look on this spot—a nation's sepulcher!
Abode of gods, whose shrines no longer burn.
Even gods must yield—religions take their turn:
'Twas Jove's—'tis Mahomet's—and other creeds
Will rise with other years, till man shall learn
Vainly his incense soars, his victim bleeds;
Poor child of Doubt and Death, whose hope is built on reeds.

4

Bound to the earth, he lifts his eye to heaven—
Is't not enough, unhappy thing! to know
Thou art? Is this a boon so kindly given,
That being, thou wouldst be again, and go,
Thou know'st not, reck'st not to what region, so
On earth no more, but mingled with the skies?
Still wilt thou dream on future joy and woe?
Regard and weigh yon dust before it flies:
That little urn saith more than thousand homilies.

5

Or burst the vanish'd Hero's lofty mound;
Far on the solitary shore he sleeps:

He fell, and falling nations mourn'd around;
But now not one of saddening thousands weeps,
Nor warlike worshipper his vigil keeps
Where demigods appear'd, as records tell.
Remove yon skull from out the scatter'd heaps:
Is that a temple where a God may dwell?
Why ev'n the worm at last disdains her shatter'd cell!

6

Look on its broken arch, its ruin'd wall,
Its chambers desolate, and portals foul:
Yes, this was once Ambition's airy hall,
The dome of Thought, the palace of the Soul:
Behold through each lackluster, eyeless hole,
The gay recess of Wisdom and of Wit
And Passion's host, that never brook'd control:
Can all, saint, sage, or sophist ever writ,
People this lonely tower, this tenement refit?

7

Well didst thou speak, Athena's wisest son!
"All that we know is, nothing can be known."
Why should we shrink from what we cannot shun?
Each has his pang, but feeble sufferers groan
With brain-born dreams of evil all their own.
Pursue what Chance or Fate proclaimeth best;
Peace waits us on the shores of Acheron:
There no forc'd banquet claims the sated guest,
But Silence spreads the couch of ever welcome rest.

24

Thus bending o'er the vessel's laving side,
To gaze on Dian's wave-reflected sphere;
The soul forgets her schemes of Hope and Pride,
And flies unconscious o'er each backward year.
None are so desolate but something dear,

Dearer than self, possesses or possess'd
A thought, and claims the homage of a tear;
A flashing pang! of which the weary breast
Would still, albeit in vain, the heavy heart divest.

25

To sit on rocks, to muse o'er flood and fell,
To slowly trace the forest's shady scene,
Where things that own not man's dominion dwell,
And mortal foot hath ne'er, or rarely been;
To climb the trackless mountain all unseen,
With the wild flock that never needs a fold;
Alone o'er steeps and foaming falls to lean;
This is not solitude; 'tis but to hold
Converse with Nature's charms, and view her stores unroll'd.

26

But midst the crowd, the hum, the shock of men,
To hear, to see, to feel, and to possess,
And roam along, the world's tir'd denizen,
With none who bless us, none whom we can bless;
Minions of splendor shrinking from distress!
None that, with kindred consciousness endued,
If we were not, would seem to smile the less
Of all that flatter'd, follow'd, sought and sued;
This is to be alone; this, this is solitude!

27

More blessed the life of godly Eremite,
Such as on lonely Athos may be seen,
Watching at Eve upon the giant height,
That looks o'er waves so blue, skies so serene,
That he who there at such an hour hath been
Will wistful linger on that hallow'd spot;
Then slowly tear him from the 'witching scene,

Sigh forth one wish that such had been his lot,
Then turn to hate a world he had almost forgot.

From CANTO III

1

Is thy face like thy mother's, my fair child!
Ada! sole daughter of my house and heart?
When last I saw thy young blue eyes they smiled,
And then we parted—not as now we part,
But with a hope—
                          Awaking with a start,
The waters heave around me; and on high
The winds lift up their voices: I depart,
Whither I know not; but the hour's gone by,
When Albion's lessening shores could grieve or glad mine eye.

2

Once more upon the waters! yet once more!
And the waves bound beneath me as a steed
That knows his rider. Welcome, to their roar!
Swift be their guidance, wheresoe'er it lead!
Though the strain'd mast should quiver as a reed,
And the rent canvas fluttering strew the gale,
Still must I on; for I am as a weed,
Flung from the rock, on Ocean's foam, to sail
Where'er the surge may sweep, or tempest's breath prevail.

3

In my youth's summer I did sing of One,
The wandering outlaw of his own dark mind;
Again I seize the theme then but begun,

And bear it with me, as the rushing wind
Bears the cloud onwards: in that Tale I find
The furrows of long thought, and dried-up tears,
Which, ebbing, leave a sterile track behind,
O'er which all heavily the journeying years
Plod the last sands of life—where not a flower appears.

4

Since my young days of passion—joy, or pain,
Perchance my heart and harp have lost a string,
And both may jar: it may be, that in vain
I would essay as I have sung to sing.
Yet, though a dreary strain, to this I cling;
So that it wean me from the weary dream
Of selfish grief or gladness—so it fling
Forgetfulness around me—it shall seem
To me, though to none else, a not ungrateful theme.

5

He, who grown aged in this world of woe,
In deeds, not years, piercing the depths of life,
So that no wonder waits him; nor below
Can love, or sorrow, fame, ambition, strife,
Cut to his heart again with the keen knife
Of silent, sharp endurance: he can tell
Why thought seeks refuge in lone caves, yet rife
With airy images, and shapes which dwell
Still unimpair'd, though old, in the soul's haunted cell.

6

'Tis to create, and in creating live
A being more intense, that we endow
With form our fancy, gaining as we give
The life we imagine, even as I do now.
What am I? Nothing; but not so art thou,
Soul of my thought! with whom I traverse earth,

Invisible but gazing, as I glow
Mix'd with thy spirit, blended with thy birth,
And feeling still with thee in my crush'd feelings' dearth.

7

Yet must I think less wildly—I *have* thought
Too long and darkly, till my brain became,
In its own eddy boiling and o'erwrought,
A whirling gulf of fantasy and flame:
And thus, untaught in youth my heart to tame,
My springs of life were poison'd. 'Tis too late!
Yet am I chang'd; though still enough the same
In strength to bear what time can not abate,
And feed on bitter fruits without accusing Fate.

8

Something too much of this—but now 'tis past,
And the spell closes with its silent seal.
Long absent HAROLD reappears at last;
He of the breast which fain no more would feel,
Wrung with the wounds which kill not, but ne'er heal;
Yet Time, who changes all, had altered him
In soul and aspect as in age: years steal
Fire from the mind as vigor from the limb;
And life's enchanted cup but sparkles near the brim.

9

His had been quaff'd too quickly, and he found
The dregs were wormwood; but he fill'd again,
And from a purer fount, on holier ground,
And deem'd its spring perpetual; but in vain!
Still round him clung invisibly a chain
Which gall'd forever, lettering though unseen,
And heavy though it clank'd not; worn with pain,
Which pined although it spoke not, and grew keen,
Entering with every step, he took, through many a scene.

10

Secure in guarded coldness, he had mix'd
Again in fancied safety with his kind,
And deem'd his spirit now so firmly fix'd
And sheath'd with an invulnerable mind,
That, if no joy, no sorrow lurk'd behind;
And he, as one, might midst the many stand
Unheeded, searching through the crowd to find
Fit speculation! such as in strange land
He found in wonderworks of God and Nature's hand.

11

But who can view the ripened rose, nor seek
To wear it? who can curiously behold
The smoothness and the sheen of beauty's cheek,
Nor feel the heart can never all grow old?
Who can contemplate Fame through clouds unfold
The star which rises o'er her steep, nor climb?
Harold, once more within the vortex, roll'd
On with the giddy circle, chasing Time,
Yet with a nobler aim than in his youth's fond prime.

12

But soon he knew himself the most unfit
Of men to herd with Man; with whom he held
Little in common; untaught to submit
His thoughts to others, though his soul was quell'd
In youth by his own thoughts; still uncompell'd,
He would not yield dominion of his mind
To spirits against whom his own rebell'd;
Proud though in desolation; which could find
A life within itself, to breathe without mankind.

13

Where rose the mountains, there to him were friends;
Where roll'd the ocean, thereon was his home;

Where a blue sky, and glowing clime, extends,
He had the passion and the power to roam;
The desert, forest, cavern, breaker's foam,
Were unto him companionship; they spake
A mutual language, clearer than the tome
Of his land's tongue, which he would oft forsake
For Nature's pages glass'd by sunbeams on the lake.

14

Like the Chaldean, he could watch the stars,
Till he had peopled them with beings bright
As their own beams; and earth, and earthborn jars,
And human frailties, were forgotten quite:
Could he have kept his spirit to that flight
He had been happy; but this clay will sink
Its spark immortal, envying it the light
To which it mounts as if to break the link
That keeps us from yon heaven which woos us to its brink.

15

But in Man's dwellings he became a thing
Restless and worn, and stern and wearisome,
Droop'd as a wild-born falcon with clipped wing,
To whom the boundless air alone were home:
Then came his fit again, which to o'ercome,
As eagerly the barr'd-up bird will beat
His breast and beak against his wiry dome
Till the blood tinge his plumage, so the heat
Of his impeded soul would through his bosom eat.

16

Self-exiled Harold wanders forth again,
With naught of hope left, but with less of gloom;
The very knowledge that he lived in vain,
That all was over on this side the tomb,

Had made Despair a smilingness assume,
Which, though 'twere wild—as on the plundered wreck
When mariners would madly meet their doom
With draughts intemperate on the sinking deck—
Did yet inspire a cheer, which he forbore to check.

17

Stop!—for thy tread is on an Empire's dust!
An Earthquake's spoil is sepulchered below!
Is the spot mark'd with no colossal bust?
Nor column trophied for triumphal show?
None; but the moral's truth tells simpler so,
As the ground was before, thus let it be—
How that red rain hath made the harvest grow!
And is this all the world has gained by thee,
Thou first and last of fields! king-making Victory?

18

And Harold stands upon this place of skulls,
The grave of France, the deadly Waterloo!
How in an hour the power which gave annuls
Its gifts, transferring fame as fleeting too!
In "pride of place" here last the eagle flew,
Then tore with bloody talon the rent plain,
Pierced by the shaft of banded nations through;
Ambition's life and labors all were vain;
He wears the shattered links of the world's broken chain.

19

Fit retribution! Gaul may champ the bit
And foam in fetters—but is Earth more free?
Did nations combat to make *One* submit;
Or league to teach all kings true sovereignty?
What! shall reviving Thraldom again be

The patched-up idol of enlightened days?
Shall we, who struck the Lion down, shall we
Pay the Wolf homage? proffering lowly gaze
And servile knees to thrones? No; *prove* before ye praise!

20

If not, o'er one fallen despot boast no more!
In vain fair cheeks were furrowed with hot tears
For Europe's flowers long rooted up before
The trampler of her vineyards; in vain years
Of death, depopulation, bondage, fears,
Have all been borne, and broken by the accord
Of roused-up millions: all that most endears
Glory, is when the myrtle wreathes a sword
Such as Harmodius drew on Athens' tyrant lord.

21

There was a sound of revelry by night,
And Belgium's capital had gathered then
Her Beauty and her Chivalry, and bright
The lamps shone o'er fair women and brave men;
A thousand hearts beat happily; and when
Music arose with its voluptuous swell,
Soft eyes look'd love to eyes which spake again,
And all went merry as a marriage bell;
But hush! hark! a deep sound strikes like a rising knell!

22

Did ye not hear it?—No; 'twas but the wind,
Or the car rattling o'er the stony street;
On with the dance! let joy be unconfined;
No sleep till morn, when Youth and Pleasure meet
To chase the glowing Hours with flying feet—
But, hark!—that heavy sound breaks in once more,
As if the clouds its echo would repeat;

And nearer, clearer, deadlier than before!
Arm! Arm! and out—it is—the cannon's opening roar!

23

Within a windowed niche of that high hall
Sate Brunswick's fated chieftain; he did hear
That sound the first amidst the festival,
And caught its tone with Death's prophetic ear;
And when they smiled because he deem'd it near,
His heart more truly knew that peal too well
Which stretch'd his father on a bloody bier,
And roused the vengeance blood alone could quell:
He rush'd into the field, and, foremost fighting, fell.

24

Ah! then and there was hurrying to and fro,
And gathering tears, and tremblings of distress,
And cheeks all pale, which but an hour ago
Blush'd at the praise of their own loveliness;
And there were sudden partings, such as press
The life from out young hearts, and choking sighs
Which ne'er might be repeated; who could guess
If ever more should meet those mutual eyes,
Since upon nights so sweet such awful morn could rise?

25

And there was mounting in hot haste: the steed,
The mustering squadron, and the clattering car,
Went pouring forward in impetuous speed,
And swiftly forming in the ranks of war;
And the deep thunder peal on peal afar;
And near, the beat of the alarming drum
Roused up the soldier ere the morning star;
While throng'd the citizens with terror dumb,
Or whispering, with white lips—"The foe! They come! they come!"

The flatterer of thy fierceness, till thou wert
A god unto thyself; nor less the same
To the astounded kingdoms all inert,
Who deem'd thee for a time whate'er thou didst assert.

38

Oh, more or less than man—in high or low,
Battling with nations, flying from the field;
Now making monarchs' necks thy footstool, now
More than thy meanest soldier taught to yield;
An empire thou couldst crush, command, rebuild,
But govern not thy pettiest passion, nor,
However deeply in men's spirits skill'd,
Look through thine own, nor curb the lust of war,
Nor learn that tempted Fate will leave the loftiest star.

39

Yet well thy soul hath brook'd the turning tide
With that untaught innate philosophy,
Which, be it wisdom, coldness, or deep pride,
Is gall and wormwood to an enemy.
When the whole-host of hatred stood hard by,
To watch and mock thee shrinking, thou hast smiled
With a sedate and all-enduring eye—
When Fortune fled her spoil'd and favorite child,
He stood unbowed beneath the ills upon him piled.

40

Sager than in thy fortunes; for in them
Ambition steel'd thee on too far to show
That just habitual scorn which could contemn
Men and their thoughts; 'twas wise to feel, not so
To wear it ever on thy lip and brow,
And spurn the instruments thou wert to use

Till they were turn'd unto thine overthrow:
'Tis but a worthless world to win or lose;
So hath it proved to thee, and all such lot who choose.

41

If, like a tower upon a headlong rock,
Thou hadst been made to stand or fall alone,
Such scorn of man had help'd to brave the shock;
But men's thoughts were the steps which paved thy throne,
Their admiration thy best weapon shone;
The part of Philip's son was thine, not then
(Unless aside thy purple had been thrown)
Like stern Diogenes to mock at men;
For sceptered cynics earth were far too wide a den.

42

But quiet to quick bosoms is a hell,
And *there* hath been thy bane; there is a fire
And motion of the soul which will not dwell
In its own narrow being, but aspire
Beyond the fitting medium of desire;
And, but once kindled, quenchless evermore,
Preys upon high adventure, nor can tire
Of aught but rest; a fever at the core,
Fatal to him who bears, to all who ever bore.

43

This makes the madmen who have made men mad
By their contagion; Conquerors and Kings,
Founders of sects and systems, to whom add
Sophists, Bards, Statesmen, all unquiet things
Which stir too strongly the soul's secret springs,
And are themselves the fools to those they fool;
Envied, yet how unenviable! what stings
Are theirs! One breast laid open were a school
Which would unteach mankind the lust to shine or rule:

44

Their breath is agitation, and their life
A storm whereon they ride, to sink at last,
And yet so nurs'd and bigoted to strife,
That should their days, surviving perils past,
Melt to calm twilight, they feel overcast
With sorrow and supineness, and so die;
Even as a flame unfed, which runs to waste
With its own flickering, or a sword laid by
Which eats into itself, and rusts ingloriously.

45

He who ascends to mountaintops, shall find
The loftiest peaks most wrapped in clouds and snow;
He who surpasses or subdues mankind,
Must look down on the hate of those below.
Though high *above* the sun of glory glow,
And far *beneath* the earth and ocean spread,
Round him are icy rocks, and loudly blow
Contending tempests on his naked head,
And thus reward the toils which to those summits led.

52

Thus Harold inly said, and pass'd along,
Yet not insensibly to all which here
Awoke the jocund birds to early song
In glens which might have made even exile dear:
Though on his brow were graven lines austere,
And tranquil sternness which had ta'en the place
Of feelings fierier far but less severe,
Joy was not always absent from his face,
But o'er it in such scenes would steal with transient trace.

53

Nor was all love shut from him, though his days
Of passion had consumed themselves to dust.

It is in vain that we would coldly gaze
On such as smile upon us; the heart must
Leap kindly back to kindness, though disgust
Hath wean'd it from all worldlings: thus he felt,
For there was soft remembrance, and sweet trust
In one fond breast, to which his own would melt,
And in its tenderer hour on that his bosom dwelt.

54

And he had learn'd to love—I know not why,
For this in such as him seems strange of mood—
The helpless looks of blooming infancy,
Even in its earliest nurture; what subdued,
To change like this, a mind so far imbued
With scorn of man, it little boots to know;
But thus it was; and though in solitude
Small power the nipp'd affections have to grow,
In him this glowed when all beside had ceased to glow.

55

And there was one soft breast, as hath been said,
Which unto his was bound by stronger ties
Than the church links withal; and, though unwed,
That love was pure, and, far above disguise,
Had stood the test of mortal enmities
Still undivided, and cemented more
By peril, dreaded most in female eyes;
But this was firm, and from a foreign shore
Well to that heart might his these absent greetings pour!

68

Lake Leman woos me with its crystal face,
The mirror where the stars and mountains view
The stillness of their aspect in each trace
Its clear depth yields of their far height and hue:

There is too much of man here, to look through
With a fit mind the might which I behold;
But soon in me shall Loneliness renew
Thoughts hid, but not less cherish'd than of old,
Ere mingling with the herd had penn'd me in their fold.

69

To fly from, need not be to hate, mankind;
All are not fit with them to stir and toil,
Nor is it discontent to keep the mind
Deep in its fountain, lest it overboil
In the hot throng, where we become the spoil
Of our infection, till too late and long
We may deplore and struggle with the coil,
In wretched interchange of wrong for wrong
'Midst a contentious world, striving where none are strong.

70

There, in a moment, we may plunge our years
In fatal penitence, and in the blight
Of our own soul, turn all our blood to tears,
And color things to come with hues of Night;
The race of life becomes a hopeless flight
To those that walk in darkness: on the sea,
The boldest steer but where their ports invite,
But there are wanderers o'er Eternity
Whose bark drives on and on, and anchored ne'er shall be.

71

Is it not better, then, to be alone,
And love Earth only for its earthly sake?
By the blue rushing of the arrowy Rhone,
Or the pure bosom of its nursing lake,
Which feeds it as a mother who doth make
A fair but froward infant her own care,

Kissing its cries away as these awake—
Is it not better thus our lives to wear,
Than join the crushing crowd, doom'd to inflict or bear?

72

I live not in myself, but I become
Portion of that around me; and to me,
High mountains are a feeling, but the hum
Of human cities torture: I can see
Nothing to loathe in nature, save to be
A link reluctant in a fleshly chain,
Class'd among creatures, when the soul can flee,
And with the sky, the peak, the heaving plain
Of ocean, or the stars, mingle, and not in vain.

73

And thus I am absorb'd, and this is life:
I look upon the peopled desert past,
As on a place of agony and strife,
Where, for some sin, to Sorrow I was cast,
To act and suffer, but remount at last
With a fresh pinion; which I feel to spring,
Though young, yet waxing vigorous, as the blast
Which it would cope with, on delighted wing,
Spurning the clay-cold bonds which round our being cling.

74

And when, at length, the mind shall be all free
From what it hates in this degraded form,
Reft of its carnal life, save what shall be
Existent happier in the fly and worm—
When elements to elements conform,
And dust is as it should be, shall I not
Feel all I see, less dazzling, but more warm?
The bodiless thought? the Spirit of each spot?
Of which, even now, I share at times the immortal lot?

75

Are not the mountains, waves, and skies, a part
Of me and of my soul, as I of them?
Is not the love of these deep in my heart
With a pure passion? should I not contemn
All objects, if compared with these? and stem
A tide of suffering, rather than forgo
Such feelings for the hard and worldly phlegm
Of those whose eyes are only turn'd below,
Gazing upon the ground, with thoughts which dare not glow?

76

But this is not my theme; and I return
To that which is immediate, and require
Those who find contemplation in the urn,
To look on One, whose dust was once all fire,
A native of the land where I respire
The clear air for a while—a passing guest,
Where he became a being—whose desire
Was to be glorious; 'twas a foolish quest,
The which to gain and keep, he sacrificed all rest.

77

Here the self-torturing sophist, wild Rousseau,
The apostle of affliction, he who threw
Enchantment over passion, and from woe
Wrung overwhelming eloquence, first drew
The breath which made him wretched; yet he knew
How to make madness beautiful, and cast
O'er erring deeds and thoughts, a heavenly hue
Of words, like sunbeams, dazzling as they past
The eyes, which o'er them shed tears feelingly and fast.

78

His love was passion's essence—as a tree
On fire by lightning; with ethereal flame

Kindled he was, and blasted; for to be
Thus, and enamored, were in him the same.
But his was not the love of living dame,
Nor of the dead who rise upon our dreams,
But of ideal beauty, which became
In him existence, and o'erflowing teems
Along his burning page, distempered though it seems.

85

Clear, placid Leman! thy contrasted lake,
With the wild world I dwelt in, is a thing
Which warns me, with its stillness, to forsake
Earth's troubled waters for a purer spring.
This quiet sail is as a noiseless wing
To waft me from distraction; once I loved
Torn ocean's roar, but thy soft murmuring
Sounds sweet as if a sister's voice reproved,
That I with stern delights should e'er have been so moved.

86

It is the hush of night, and all between
Thy margin and the mountains, dusk, yet clear,
Mellowed and mingling, yet distinctly seen,
Save darken'd Jura, whose capped heights appear
Precipitously steep; and drawing near,
There breathes a living fragrance from the shore,
Of flowers yet fresh with childhood; on the ear
Drops the light drip of the suspended oar,
Or chirps the grasshopper one goodnight carol more;

87

He is an evening reveler, who makes
His life an infancy, and sings his fill;
At intervals, some bird from out the brakes,
Starts into voice a moment, then is still.

There seems a floating whisper on the hill,
But that is fancy, for the starlight dews
All silently their tears of love instill,
Weeping themselves away, till they infuse
Deep into Nature's breast the spirit of her hues.

88

Ye stars! which are the poetry of heaven!
If in your bright leaves we would read the fate
Of men and empires—'tis to be forgiven,
That in our aspirations to be great,
Our destinies o'erleap their mortal state,
And claim a kindred with you; for ye are
A beauty and a mystery, and create
In us such love and reverence from afar,
That fortune, fame, power, life, have named themselves a star.

89

All heaven and earth are still—though not in sleep,
But breathless, as we grow when feeling most;
And silent, as we stand in thoughts too deep—
All heaven and earth are still: From the high host
Of stars, to the lull'd lake and mountain coast,
All is concentered in a life intense,
Where not a beam, nor air, nor leaf is lost,
But hath a part of being, and a sense
Of that which is of all Creator and defense.

90

Then stirs the feeling infinite, so felt
In solitude, where we are *least* alone;
A truth, which through our being then doth melt
And purifies from self: it is a tone,
The soul and source of music, which makes known
Eternal harmony, and sheds a charm,

Like to the fabled Cytherea's zone,
Binding all things with beauty—'twould disarm
The specter Death, had he substantial power to harm.

91

Not vainly did the early Persian make
His altar the high places and the peak
Or earth-o'ergazing mountains, and thus take
A fit and unwall'd temple, there to seek
The Spirit, in whose honor shrines are weak,
Uprear'd of human hands. Come, and compare
Columns and idol-dwellings, Goth or Greek,
With Nature's realms of worship, earth and air,
Nor fix on fond abodes to circumscribe thy prayer!

92

The sky is changed!—and such a change! Oh night,
And storm, and darkness, ye are wondrous strong,
Yet lovely in your strength, as is the light
Of a dark eye in woman! Far along,
From peak to peak, the rattling crags among
Leaps the live thunder! Not from one lone cloud,
But every mountain now hath found a tongue,
And Jura answers, through her misty shroud,
Back to the joyous Alps, who call to her aloud!

93

And this is in the night—Most glorious night!
Thou wert not sent for slumber! let me be
A sharer in thy fierce and far delight—
A portion of the tempest and of thee!
How the lit lake shines, a phosphoric sea,
And the big rain comes dancing to the earth!
And now again 'tis black—and now, the glee
Of the loud hills shakes with its mountain-mirth,
As if they did rejoice o'er a young earthquake's birth.

94

Now, where the swift Rhone cleaves his way between
Heights which appear as lovers who have parted
In hate, whose mining depths so intervene,
That they can meet no more, though brokenhearted;
Though in their souls, which thus each other thwarted,
Love was the very root of the fond rage
Which blighted their life's bloom, and then departed—
Itself expired, but leaving them an age
Of years all winters—war within themselves to wage.

95

Now, where the quick Rhone thus hath cleft his way,
The mightiest of the storms hath ta'en his stand:
For here, not one, but many, make their play,
And fling their thunderbolts from hand to hand,
Flashing and cast around: of all the band,
The brightest through these parted hills hath fork'd
His lightnings—as if he did understand,
That in such gaps as desolation work'd,
There the hot shaft should blast whatever therein lurk'd.

96

Sky, mountains, river, winds, lake, lightnings! ye!
With night, and clouds, and thunder, and a soul
To make these felt and feeling, well may be
Things that have made me watchful; the far roll
Of your departing voices, is the knoll
Of what in me is sleepless—if I rest.
But where of ye, oh tempests! is the goal?
Are ye like those within the human breast?
Or do ye find, at length, like eagles, some high nest?

97

Could I embody and unbosom now
That which is most within me—could I wreak

My thoughts upon expression, and thus throw
Soul, heart, mind, passions, feelings, strong or weak,
All that I would have sought, and all I seek,
Bear, know, feel, and yet breathe—into *one* word,
And that one word were Lightning, I would speak;
But as it is, I live and die unheard,
With a most voiceless thought, sheathing it as a sword.

98

The morn is up again, the dewy morn,
With breath all incense, and with cheek all bloom,
Laughing the clouds away with playful scorn,
And living as if earth contain'd no tomb—
And glowing into day: we may resume
The march of our existence: and thus I,
Still on thy shores, fair Leman! may find room
And food for meditation, nor pass by
Much, that may give us pause, if pondered fittingly.

113

I have not loved the world, nor the world me;
I have not flattered its rank breath, nor bow'd
To its idolatries a patient knee—
Nor coin'd my cheek to smiles—nor cried aloud
In worship of an echo; in the crowd
They could not deem me one of such; I stood
Among them, but not of them; in a shroud
Of thoughts which were not their thoughts, and still could,
Had I not filed my mind, which thus itself subdued.

114

I have not loved the world, nor the world me—
But let us part fair foes; I do believe,
Though I have found them not, that there may be
Words which are things—hopes which will not deceive,

And virtues which are merciful, nor weave
Snares for the failing: I would also deem
O'er others' griefs that some sincerely grieve;
That two, or one, are almost what they seem—
That goodness is no name, and happiness no dream.

115

My daughter! with thy name this song begun—
My daughter! with thy name thus much shall end—
I see thee not—I hear thee not—but none
Can be so wrapped in thee; thou art the friend
To whom the shadows of far years extend:
Albeit my brow thou never should'st behold,
My voice shall with thy future visions blend,
And reach into thy heart—when mine is cold—
A token and a tone, even from thy father's mold.

116

To aid thy mind's development—to watch
Thy dawn of little joys—to sit and see
Almost thy very growth—to view thee catch
Knowledge of objects—wonders yet to thee!
To hold thee lightly on a gentle knee,
And print on thy soft cheek a parent's kiss—
This, it should seem, was not reserv'd for me;
Yet this was in my nature—as it is,
I know not what is there, yet something like to this.

117

Yet, though dull Hate as duty should be taught,
I know that thou wilt love me; though my name
Should be shut from thee, as a spell still fraught
With desolation—and a broken claim:
Though the grave closed between us—'twere the same,
I know that thou wilt love me; though to drain

My blood from out thy being, were an aim,
And an attainment—all would be in vain—
Still thou would'st love me, still that more than life retain.

118

The child of love—though born in bitterness,
And nurtured in convulsion—of thy sire
These were the elements—and thine no less.
As yet such are around thee—but thy fire
Shall be more tempered, and thy hope far higher.
Sweet be thy cradled slumbers! O'er the sea,
And from the mountains where I now respire,
Fain would I waft such blessing upon thee,
As, with a sigh, I deem thou might'st have been to me!

From CANTO IV

1

I stood in Venice, on the Bridge of Sighs;
A palace and a prison on each hand:
I saw from out the wave her structures rise
As from the stroke of the enchanter's wand:
A thousand years their cloudy wings expand
Around me, and a dying Glory smiles
O'er the far times, when many a subject land
Look'd to the winged Lion's marble piles,
Where Venice sate in state, thron'd on her hundred isles!

2

She looks a sea Cybele, fresh from ocean,
Rising with her tiara of proud towers
At airy distance, with majestic motion,
A ruler of the waters and their powers:

And such she was—her daughters had their dowers
From spoils of nations, and the exhaustless East
Pour'd in her lap all gems in sparkling showers.
In purple was she robed, and of her feast
Monarchs partook, and deem'd their dignity increas'd.

3

In Venice Tasso's echoes are no more,
And silent rows the songless gondolier;
Her palaces are crumbling to the shore,
And music meets not always now the ear:
Those days are gone—but Beauty still is here.
States fall, arts fade—but Nature doth not die,
Nor yet forget how Venice once was dear,
The pleasant place of all festivity,
The revel of the earth, the masque of Italy!

4

But unto us she hath a spell beyond
Her name in story, and her long array
Of might shadows, whose dim forms despond
Above the dogeless city's vanish'd sway;
Ours is a trophy which will not decay
With the Rialto; Shylock and the Moor,
And Pierre, can not be swept or worn away—
The keystones of the arch! though all were o'er,
For us repeopled were the solitary shore.

5

The beings of the mind are not of clay;
Essentially immortal, they create
And multiply in us a brighter ray
And more beloved existence: that which Fate
Prohibits to dull life, in this our state
Of mortal bondage, by these spirits supplied
First exiles, then replaces what we hate;

Watering the heart whose early flowers have died,
And with a fresher growth replenishing the void.

6

Such is the refuge of our youth and age,
The first from Hope, the last from Vacancy;
And this worn feeling peoples many a page;
And, may be, that which grows beneath mine eye:
Yet there are things whose strong reality
Outshines our fairyland; in shape and hues
More beautiful than our fantastic sky,
And the strange constellations which the Muse
O'er her wild universe is skillful to diffuse:

7

I saw or dreamed of such—but let them go—
They came like truth, and disappeared like dreams;
And whatsoe'er they were—are now but so:
I could replace them if I would, still teems
My mind with many a form which aptly seems
Such as I sought for, and at moments found;
Let these too go—for waking Reason deems
Such overweening fantasies unsound,
And other voices speak, and other sights surround.

93

What from this barren being do we reap?
Our senses narrow, and our reason frail,
Life short, and truth a gem which loves the deep,
And all things weigh'd in custom's falsest scale;
Opinion an omnipotence—whose veil
Mantles the earth with darkness, until right
And wrong are accidents, and men grow pale
Lest their own judgments should become too bright,
And their free thoughts be crimes, and earth have too much light.

94

And thus they plod in sluggish misery,
Rotting from sire to son, and age to age,
Proud of their trampled nature, and so die,
Bequeathing their hereditary rage
To the new race of inborn slaves, who wage
War for their chains, and rather than be free,
Bleed gladiator-like, and still engage
Within the same arena where they see
Their fellows fall before, like leaves of the same tree.

95

I speak not of men's creeds—they rest between
Man and his Maker—but of things allowed,
Averr'd, and known—and daily, hourly seen—
The yoke that is upon us doubly bowed,
And the intent of tyranny avowed,
The edict of Earth's rulers, who are grown
The apes of him who humbled once the proud,
And shook them from their slumbers on the throne;
Too glorious, were this all his mighty arm had done.

96

Can tyrants but by tyrants conquered be,
And Freedom find no champion and no child
Such as Columbia saw arise when she
Sprung forth a Pallas, armed and undefiled?
Or must such minds be nourished in the wild,
Deep in the unpruned forest, 'midst the roar
Of cataracts, where nursing Nature smiled
On infant Washington? Has Earth no more
Such seeds within her breast, or Europe no such shore?

97

But France got drunk with blood to vomit crime,
And fatal have her Saturnalia been

To Freedom's cause, in every age and clime;
Because the deadly days which we have seen,
And vile Ambition, that built up between
Man and his hopes an adamantine wall,
And the base pageant last upon the scene,
Are grown the pretext for the eternal thrall
Which nips life's tree, and dooms man's worst—his second fall.

98

Yet, Freedom! yet thy banner, torn, but flying,
Streams like the thunderstorm *against* the wind;
Thy trumpet voice, though broken now and dying,
The loudest still the tempest leaves behind;
Thy tree hath lost its blossoms, and the rind,
Chopp'd by the ax, looks rough and little worth,
But the sap lasts—and still the seed we find
Sown deep, even in the bosom of the North;
So shall a better spring less bitter fruit bring forth.

99

There is a stern round tower of other days,
Firm as a fortress, with its fence of stone,
Such as an army's baffled strength delays,
Standing with half its battlements alone,
And with two thousand years of ivy grown,
The garland of eternity, where wave
The green leaves over all by time o'erthrown—
What was this tower of strength? within its cave
What treasure lay so lock'd, so hid?—A woman's grave.

100

But who was she, the lady of the dead,
Tombed in a palace? Was she chaste and fair?
Worthy a king's—or more—a Roman's bed?
What race of chiefs and heroes did she bear?

What daughter of her beauties was the heir?
How lived—how loved—how died she? Was she not
So honored—and conspicuously there,
Where meaner relics must not dare to rot,
Placed to commemorate a more than mortal lot?

101

Was she as those who love their lords, or they
Who love the lords of others? such have been,
Even in the olden time Rome's annals say.
Was she a matron of Cornelia's mien,
Or the light air of Egypt's graceful queen,
Profuse of joy—or 'gainst it did she war,
Inveterate in virtue? Did she lean
To the soft side of the heart, or wisely bar
Love from amongst her griefs?—for such the affections are.

102

Perchance she died in youth: it may be, bowed
With woes far heavier than the ponderous tomb
That weighed upon her gentle dust, a cloud
Might gather o'er her beauty, and a gloom
In her dark eye, prophetic of the doom
Heaven gives its favorites—early death; yet shed
A sunset charm around her, and illume
With hectic light, the Hesperus of the dead,
Of her consuming cheek the autumnal leaflike red.

103

Perchance she died in age—surviving all,
Charms, kindred, children—with the silver gray
On her long tresses, which might yet recall,
It may be, still a something of the day
When they were braided, and her proud array
And lovely form were envied, praised, and eyed

By Rome—But whither would Conjecture stray?
Thus much alone we know—Metella died,
The wealthiest Roman's wife; Behold his love or pride!

104

I know not why—but standing thus by thee
It seems as if I had thine inmate known,
Thou tomb! and other days come back on me
With recollected music, though the tone
Is changed and solemn, like the cloudy groan
Of dying thunder on the distant wind;
Yet could I seat me by this ivied stone
Till I had bodied forth the heated mind
Forms from the floating wreck which Ruin leaves behind;

105

And from the planks, far shattered o'er the rocks,
Built me a little bark of hope, once more
To battle with the ocean and the shocks
Of the loud breakers, and the ceaseless roar
Which rushes on the solitary shore
Where all lies foundered that was ever dear:
But could I gather from the wave-worn store
Enough for my rude boat, where should I steer?
There woos no home, nor hope, nor life, save what is here.

106

Then let the winds howl on! their harmony
Shall henceforth be my music, and the night
The sound shall temper with the owlet's cry,
As I now hear them, in the fading light
Dim o'er the bird of darkness' native site,
Answering each other on the Palatine,
With their large eyes, all glistening gray and bright,
And sailing pinions—Upon such a shrine
What are our petty griefs?—let me not number mine.

107

Cypress and ivy, weed and wallflower grown
Matted and mass'd together, hillocks heap'd
On what were chambers, arch crush'd, column strown
In fragments, chok'd up vaults, and frescoes steep'd
In subterranean damps, where the owl peep'd,
Deeming it midnight—Temples, baths, or halls?
Pronounce who can; for all that Learning reap'd
From her research hath been, that these are walls—
Behold the Imperial Mount! 'tis thus the mighty falls.

108

There is the moral of all human tales;
'Tis but the same rehearsal of the past,
First Freedom, and then Glory—when that fails,
Wealth, vice, corruption—barbarism at last.
And History, with all her volumes vast,
Hath but *one* page—'tis better written here,
Where gorgeous Tyranny had thus amass'd
All treasures, all delights, that eye or ear,
Heart, soul could seek, tongue ask—Away with words! draw near,

109

Admire, exult—despise—laugh, weep—for here
There is such matter for all feeling—Man!
Thou pendulum betwixt a smile and tear,
Ages and realms are crowded in this span,
This mountain, whose obliterated plan
The pyramid of empires pinnacled,
Of Glory's gewgaws shining in the van
Till the sun's rays with added flame were fill'd!
Where are its golden roofs? where those who dared to build?

110

Tully was not so eloquent as thou,
Thou nameless column with the buried base!

What are the laurels of the Caesar's brow?
Crown me with ivy from his dwelling place.
Whose arch or pillar meets me in the face,
Titus or Trajan's? No—'tis that of Time:
Triumph, arch, pillar, all he doth displace
Scoffing; and apostolic statues climb
To crush the imperial urn, whose ashes slept sublime,

111

Buried in air, the deep blue sky of Rome,
And looking to the stars: they had contain'd
A spirit which with these would find a home,
The last of those who o'er the whole earth reign'd,
The Roman globe, for after none sustain'd,
But yielded back his conquests—he was more
Than a mere Alexander, and, unstain'd
With household blood and wine, serenely wore
His sovereign virtues—still we Trajan's name adore.

115

Egeria! sweet creation of some heart
Which found no mortal resting place so fair
As thine ideal breast; whate'er thou art
Or wert—a young Aurora of the air,
The nympholepsy of some fond despair;
Or, it might be, a beauty of the earth,
Who found a more than common votary there
Too much adoring; whatso'er thy birth,
Thou wert a beautiful thought, and softly bodied forth.

116

The mosses of thy fountain still are sprinkled
With thine Elysian waterdrops; the face
Of thy cave-guarded spring, with years unwrinkled,
Reflects the meek-eyed genius of the place,

Art's works; nor must the delicate waters sleep,
Whose green, wild margin now no more erase
Art's works; nor must the delicate waters sleep,
Prisoned in marble, bubbling from the base
Of the cleft statue, with a gentle leap
The rill runs o'er, and round, fern, flowers, and ivy, creep,

117

Fantastically tangled; the green hills
Are clothed with early blossoms, through the grass
The quick-eyed lizard rustles, and the bills
Of summer birds sing welcome as ye pass;
Flowers fresh in hue, and many in their class,
Implore the pausing step, and with their dyes
Dance in the soft breeze in a fairy mass;
The sweetness of the violet's deep blue eyes,
Kiss'd by the breath of heaven, seems colored by its skies.

118

Here didst thou dwell, in this enchanted cover,
Egeria! thy all heavenly bosom beating
For the far footsteps of thy mortal lover;
The purple Midnight veil'd that mystic meeting
With her most starry canopy, and seating
Thyself by thine adorer, what befell?
This cave was surely shaped out for the greeting
Of an enamor'd Goddess, and the cell
Haunted by holy Love—the earliest oracle!

119

And didst thou not, thy breast to his replying,
Blend a celestial with a human heart;
And Love, which dies as it was born, in sighing,
Share with immortal transports? could thine art
Make them indeed immortal, and impart

The purity of heaven to earthly joys,
Expel the venom and not blunt the dart—
The dull satiety which all destroys—
And root from out the soul the deadly weed which cloys?

120

Alas! our young affections run to waste,
Or water but the desert; whence arise
But weeds of dark luxuriance, tares of haste,
Rank at the core, though tempting to the eyes,
Flowers whose wild odors breathe but agonies,
And trees whose gums are poison; such the plants
Which spring beneath her steps as Passion flies
O'er the world's wilderness, and vainly pants
For some celestial fruit forbidden to our wants.

121

Oh Love! no habitant of earth thou art—
An unseen seraph, we believe in thee,
A faith whose martyrs are the broken heart,
But never yet hath seen, nor e'er shall see
The naked eye, thy form, as it should be;
The mind hath made thee, as it peopled heaven,
Even with its own desiring fantasy,
And to a thought such shape and image given,
As haunts the unquench'd soul—parch'd—wearied—wrung
    —and riven.

122

Of its own beauty is the mind diseased,
And fevers into false creation—where,
Where are the forms the sculptor's soul hath seized?
In him alone. Can Nature show so fair?
Where are the charms and virtues which we dare
Conceive in boyhood and pursue as men,

The unreach'd Paradise of our despair,
Which o'er-informs the pencil and the pen,
And overpowers the page where it would bloom again?

123

Who loves, raves—'tis youth's frenzy—but the cure
Is bitterer still; as charm by charm unwinds
Which robed our idols, and we see too sure
Nor worth nor beauty dwells from out the mind's
Ideal shape of such; yet still it binds
The fatal spell, and still it draws us on,
Reaping the whirlwind from the oft-sown winds;
The stubborn heart, its alchemy begun,
Seems ever near the prize—wealthiest when most undone.

124

We wither from our youth, we gasp away—
Sick—sick; unfound the boon—unslaked the thirst,
Though to the last, in verge of our decay,
Some phantom lures, such as we sought at first—
But all too late—so are we doubly cursed.
Love, fame, ambition, avarice—'tis the same,
Each idle—and all ill—and none the worst—
For all are meteors with a different name,
And Death the sable smoke where vanishes the flame.

125

Few—none—find what they love or could have loved,
Though accident, blind contact, and the strong
Necessity of loving, have removed
Antipathies—but to recur, ere long,
Envenomed with irrevocable wrong;
And Circumstance, that unspiritual god
And miscreator, makes and helps along
Our coming evils with a crutchlike rod,
Whose touch turns Hope to dust—the dust we all have trod.

126

Our life is a false nature—'tis not in
The harmony of things—this hard decree,
This uneradicable taint of sin,
This boundless upas, this all-blasting tree,
Whose root is earth, whose leaves and branches be
The skies which rain their plagues on men like dew—
Disease, death, bondage—all the woes we see—
And worse, the woes we see not—which throb through
The immedicable soul, with heartaches ever new.

127

Yet let us ponder boldly—'tis a base
Abandonment of reason to resign
Our right of thought—our last and only place
Of refuge; this, at least, shall still be mine:
Though from our birth the faculty divine
Is chain'd and tortured—cabin'd, cribb'd, confined,
And bred in darkness, lest the truth should shine
Too brightly on the unprepared mind,
The beam pours in, for time and skill will couch the blind.

128

Arches on arches! as it were that Rome,
Collecting the chief trophies of her line,
Would build up all her triumphs in one dome,
Her Coliseum stands; the moonbeams shine
As 'twere its natural torches, for divine
Should be the light which streams here, to illume
This long-explored but still exhaustless mine
Of contemplation; and the azure gloom
Of an Italian night, where the deep skies assume

129

Hues which have words, and speak to ye of heaven,
Floats o'er this vast and wondrous monument,

And shadows forth its glory. There is given
Unto the things of earth, which time hath bent,
A spirit's feeling, and where he hath leant
His hand, but broke his scythe, there is a power
And magic in the ruined battlement,
For which the palace of the present hour
Must yield its pomp, and wait till ages are its dower.

130

Oh Time! the beautifier of the dead,
Adorner of the ruin, comforter
And only healer when the heart hath bled—
Time! the corrector where our judgments err,
The test of truth, love—sole philosopher,
For all beside are sophists, from thy thrift,
Which never loses though it doth defer—
Time, the avenger! unto thee I lift
My hands, and eyes, and heart, and crave for thee a gift:

131

Amidst this wreck, where thou hast made a shrine
And temple more divinely desolate,
Among thy mightier offerings here are mine,
Ruins of years—though few, yet full of fate—
If thou hast ever seen me too elate,
Hear me not; but if calmly I have borne
Good, and reserved my pride against the hate
Which shall not whelm me, let me not have worn
This iron in my soul in vain—shall *they* not mourn?

132

And thou, who never yet of human wrong
Left'st the unbalanced scale, great Nemesis!
Here, where the ancient paid thee homage long—
Thou, who didst call the Furies from the abyss,
And round Orestes bade them howl and hiss

For that unnatural retribution—just,
Had it but been from hands less near—in this
Thy former realm, I call thee from the dust!
Dost thou not hear my heart?—Awake! thou shalt, and must.

133

It is not that I may not have incurr'd
For my ancestral faults or mine the wound
I bleed withal, and, had it been conferr'd
With a just weapon, it had flowed unbound;
But now my blood shall not sink in the ground;
To thee I do devote it—*thou* shalt take
The vengeance, which shall yet be sought and found,
Which if *I* have not taken for the sake—
But let that pass—I sleep, but thou shalt yet awake.

134

And if my voice break forth, 'tis not that now
I shrink from what is suffered: let him speak
Who hath beheld decline upon my brow,
Or seen my mind's convulsion leave it weak;
But in this page a record will I seek.
Not in the air shall these my words disperse,
Though I be ashes; a far hour shall wreak
The deep prophetic fullness of this verse,
And pile on human heads the mountain of my curse!

135

That curse shall be Forgiveness—Have I not—
Hear me, my mother Earth! behold it, Heaven!—
Have I not had to wrestle with my lot?
Have I not suffered things to be forgiven?
Have I not had my brain seared, my heart riven,
Hopes sapp'd, name blighted, Life's life lied away?
And only not to desperation driven,

Because not altogether of such clay
As rots into the souls of those whom I survey.

136

From mighty wrongs to petty perfidy
Have I not seen what human things could do?
From the loud roar of foaming calumny
To the small whisper of the as paltry few,
And subtler venom of the reptile crew,
The Janus glance of whose significant eye,
Learning to lie with silence, would *seem* true,
And without utterance, save the shrug or sigh,
Deal round to happy fools its speechless obloquy.

137

But I have lived, and have not lived in vain:
My mind may lose its force, my blood its fire,
And my frame perish even in conquering pain,
But there is that within me which shall tire
Torture and Time, and breathe when I expire;
Something unearthly, which they deem not of,
Like the remembered tone of a mute lyre,
Shall on their softened spirits sink, and move
In hearts all rocky now the late remorse of love.

138

The seal is set—Now welcome, thou dread power
Nameless, yet thus omnipotent, which here
Walk'st in the shadow of the midnight hour
With a deep awe, yet all distinct from fear;
Thy haunts are ever where the dead walls rear
Their ivy mantles, and the solemn scene
Derives from thee a sense so deep and clear
That we become a part of what has been,
And grow unto the spot, all-seeing but unseen.

139

And here the buzz of eager nations ran,
In murmured pity, or loud-roared applause,
As man was slaughtered by his fellow man.
And wherefore slaughtered? wherefore, but because
Such were the bloody Circus' genial laws,
And the imperial pleasure—Wherefore not?
What matters where we fall to fill the maws
Of worms—on battle plains or listed spot?
Both are but theaters where the chief actors rot.

140

I see before me the Gladiator lie:
He leans upon his hand—his manly brow
Consents to death, but conquers agony,
And his drooped head sinks gradually low—
And through his side the last drops, ebbing slow
From the red gash, fall heavy, one by one,
Like the first of a thundershower; and now
The arena swims around him—he is gone,
Ere ceased the inhuman shout which hail'd the wretch who won.

141

He heard it, but he heeded not—his eyes
Were with his heart, and that was far away;
He reck'd not of the life he lost nor prize,
But where his rude hut by the Danube lay
There were his young barbarians all at play,
There was their Dacian mother—he, their sire,
Butcher'd to make a Roman holiday—
All this rush'd with his blood—Shall he expire
And unavenged?—Arise! ye Goths, and glut your ire!

142

But here, where Murder breathed her bloody stream;
And here, where buzzing nations choked the ways,

And roar'd or murmur'd like a mountain stream
Dashing or winding as its torrent strays;
Here, where the Roman million's blame or praise
Was death or life, the playthings of a crowd,
My voice sounds much—and fall the stars' faint rays
On the arena void—seats crush'd—walls bow'd—
And galleries, where my steps seem echoes strangely loud.

143

A ruin—yet what ruin! from its mass
Walls, palaces, half-cities, have been reared;
Yet oft the enormous skeleton ye pass
And marvel where the spoil could have appeared,
Hath it indeed been plundered, or but cleared?
Alas! developed, opens the decay,
When the colossal fabric's form is neared:
It will not bear the brightness of the day,
Which streams too much on all years, man, have reft away.

144

But when the rising moon begins to climb
Its topmost arch, and gently pauses there;
When the stars twinkle through the loops of time,
And the low night breeze waves along the air
The garland forest, which the gray walls wear,
Like laurels on the bald first Caesar's head;
When the light shines serene but doth not glare,
Then in this magic circle raise the dead:
Heroes have trod this spot—'tis on their dust ye tread.

145

"While stands the Coliseum, Rome shall stand;
When falls the Coliseum, Rome shall fall;
And when Rome falls—the World." From our own land
Thus spake the pilgrims o'er this mighty wall

In Saxon times, which we are wont to call
Ancient; and these three mortal things are still
On their foundations, and unaltered all;
Rome and her Ruin past Redemption's skill,
The World, the same wide den—of thieves, or what ye will.

155

Enter: its grandeur overwhelms thee not;
And why? it is not lessened; but thy mind,
Expanded by the genius of the spot,
Has grown colossal, and can only find
A fit abode wherein appear enshrined
Thy hopes of immortality; and thou
Shalt one day, if found worthy, so defined,
See thy God face to face, as thou dost now
His Holy of Holies, nor be blasted by his brow.

156

Thou movest—but increasing with the advance,
Like climbing some great Alp, which still doth rise,
Deceived by its gigantic elegance;
Vastness which grows—but grows to harmonize—
All musical in its immensities;
Rich marbles—richer painting—shrines where flame
The lamps of gold—and haughty dome which vies
In air with Earth's chief structures, though their frame
Sits on the firm-set ground—and this the clouds must claim

157

Thou seest not all; but piecemeal thou must break,
To separate contemplation, the great whole;
And as the ocean many bays will make,
That ask the eye—so here condense thy soul
To more immediate objects, and control
Thy thoughts until thy mind hath got by heart

Its eloquent proportions, and unroll
In mighty graduations, part by part,
The glory which at once upon thee did not dart,

158

Not by its fault—but thine: Our outward sense
Is but of gradual grasp—and as it is
That what we have of feeling most intense
Outstrips our faint expression; even so this
Outshining and o'erwhelming edifice
Fools our fond gaze, and greatest of the great
Defies at first our Nature's littleness,
Till, growing with its growth, we thus dilate
Our spirits to the size of that they contemplate.

159

Then pause, and be enlightened; there is more
In such a survey than the sating gaze
Of wonder please, or awe which would adore
The worship of the place, or the mere praise
Of art and its great masters, who could raise
What former time, nor skill, nor thought could plan;
The fountain of sublimity displays
Its depth, and thence may draw the mind of man
Its golden sands, and learn what great conceptions can.

160

Or, turning to the Vatican, go see
Laocoon's torture dignifying pain—
A father's love and mortal's agony
With an immortal's patience blending—Vain
The struggle; vain, against the coiling strain
And gripe, and deepening of the dragon's grasp,
The old man's clench; the long envenomed chain
Rivets the living links—the enormous asp
Enforces pang on pang, and stifles gasp on gasp.

161

Or view the Lord of the unerring bow,
The God of life, and poesy, and light—
The Sun in human limbs arrayed, and brow
All radiant from his triumph in the fight;
The shaft hath just been shot—the arrow bright
With an immortal's vengeance; in his eye
And nostril beautiful disdain, and might,
And majesty, flash their full lightnings by,
Developing in that one glance the Deity.

162

But in his delicate form—a dream of Love,
Shaped by some solitary nymph, whose breast
Long'd for a deathless lover from above,
And madden'd in that vision—are expressed
All that ideal beauty ever bless'd
The mind within its most unearthly mood,
When each conception was a heavenly guest—
A ray of immortality—and stood,
Starlike, around, until they gathered to a god!

163

And if it be Prometheus stole from Heaven
The fire which we endure, it was repaid
By him to whom the energy was given
Which this poetic marble hath array'd
With an eternal glory—which, if made
By human hands, is not of human thought;
And Time himself hath hallowed it, nor laid
One ringlet in the dust—nor hath it caught
A tinge of years, but breathes the flame with which 'twas
     wrought.

175

But I forget—My pilgrim's shrine is won,
And he and I must part—so let it be—

His task and mine alike are nearly done;
Yet once more let us look upon the sea;
The midland ocean breaks on him and me,
And from the Alban Mount we now behold
Our friend of youth, that ocean, which when we
Beheld it last by Calpe's rock unfold
Those waves, we followed on till the dark Euxine roll'd

176

Upon the blue Symplegades: long years—
Long, though not very many, since have done
Their work on both; some suffering and some tears
Have left us nearly where we had begun:
Yet not in vain our mortal race hath run,
We have had our reward—and it is here;
That we can yet feel gladden'd by the sun,
And reap from earth, sea, joy almost as dear
As if there were no man to trouble what is clear.

177

Oh! that the Desert were my dwelling place,
With one fair Spirit for my minister,
That I might all forget the human race,
And, hating no one, love but only her!
Ye Elements!—in whose ennobling stir
I feel myself exalted—Can ye not
Accord me such a being? Do I err
In deeming such inhabit many a spot?
Though with them to converse can rarely be our lot.

178

There is a pleasure in the pathless woods,
There is a rapture on the lonely shore,
There is society, where none intrudes,
By the deep Sea, and music in its roar:

I love not Man the less, but Nature more,
From these our interviews, in which I steal
From all I may be, or have been before,
To mingle with the Universe, and feel
What I can ne'er express, yet can not all conceal.

179

Roll on, thou deep and dark blue ocean—roll!
Ten thousand fleets sweep over thee in vain;
Man marks the earth with ruin—his control
Stops with the shore—upon the watery plain
The wrecks are all thy deed, nor doth remain
A shadow of man's ravage, save his own,
When, for a moment, like a drop of rain,
He sinks into thy depths with bubbling groan,
Without a grave, unknell'd, uncoffin'd, and unknown.

180

His steps are not upon thy paths—thy fields
Are not a spoil for him—thou dost arise
And shake him from thee; the vile strength he wields
For earth's destruction thou dost all despise,
Spurning him from thy bosom to the skies,
And send'st him, shivering in thy playful spray
And howling, to his Gods, where haply lies
His petty hope in some near port or bay,
And dashest him again to earth—there let him lay.

181

The armaments which thunderstrike the walls
Of rock-built cities, bidding nations quake,
And monarchs tremble in their capitals,
The oak leviathans, whose huge ribs make
Their clay creator the vain title take
Of lord of thee, and arbiter of war;

These are thy toys, and, as the snowy flake,
They melt into thy yeast of waves, which mar
Alike the Armada's pride, or spoils of Trafalgar.

182

Thy shores are empires, changed in all save thee—
Assyria, Greece, Rome, Carthage, what are they?
Thy waters washed them power while they were free,
And many a tyrant since; their shores obey
The stranger, slave, or savage; their decay
Has dried up realms to deserts—not so thou,
Unchangeable save to thy wild waves' play—
Time writes no wrinkle on thine azure brow—
Such as creation's dawn beheld, thou rollest now.

183

Thou glorious mirror, where the Almighty's form
Glasses itself in tempests; in all time,
Calm or convuls'd—in breeze, or gale, or storm,
Icing the pole, or in the torrid clime
Dark-heaving—boundless, endless, and sublime—
The image of Eternity—the throne
Of the Invisible, even from out thy slime
The monsters of the deep are made; each zone
Obeys thee; thou goest forth, dread, fathomless, alone.

184

And I have loved thee, Ocean! and my joy
Of youthful sports was on thy breast to be
Borne, like thy bubbles, onward: from a boy
I wantoned with thy breakers—they to me
Were a delight; and if the freshening sea
Made them a terror—'twas a pleasing fear,
For I was as it were a child of thee,
And trusted to thy billows far and near,
And laid my hand upon thy mane—as I do here.

185

My task is done—my song hath ceased—my theme
Has died into an echo; it is fit
The spell should break of this protracted dream.
The torch shall be extinguish'd which hath lit
My midnight lamp—and what is writ, is writ—
Would it were worthier! but I am not now
That which I have been—and my visions flit
Less palpably before me—and the glow
Which in my spirit dwelt, is fluttering, faint, and low.

186

Farewell! a word that must be, and hath been—
A sound which makes us linger—yet—farewell!
Ye! who have traced the Pilgrim to the scene
Which is his last, if in your memories dwell
A thought which once was his, if on ye swell
A single recollection, not in vain
He wore his sandal-shoon, and scallop shell;
Farewell! with *him* alone may rest the pain,
If such there were—with *you*, the moral of his strain!

The Vision of
Judgment

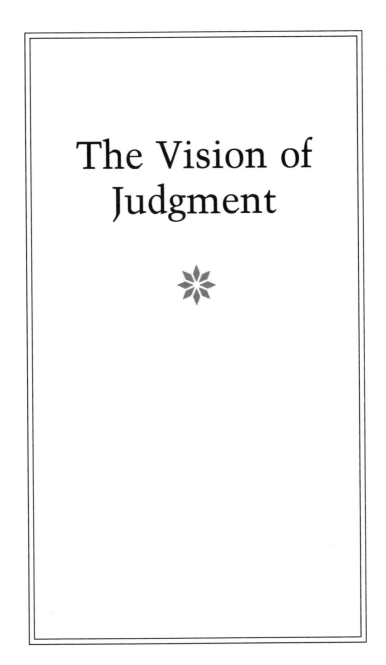

THE VISION OF JUDGMENT

1

Saint Peter sat by the celestial gate,
　His keys were rusty, and the lock was dull,
So little trouble had been given of late;
　Not that the place by any means was full,
But since the Gallic era "eighty-eight,"
　The devils had ta'en a longer, stronger pull,
And "a pull altogether," as they say
At sea—which drew most souls another way.

2

The angels all were singing out of tune,
　And hoarse with having little else to do,
Excepting to wind up the sun and moon,
　Or curb a runaway young star or two,
Or wild colt of a comet, which too soon
　Broke out of bounds o'er the ethereal blue,
Splitting some planet with its playful tail,
As boats are sometimes by a wanton whale.

3

The guardian seraphs had retired on high,
　Finding their charges past all care below;
Terrestrial business fill'd naught in the sky
　Save the recording angel's black bureau;
Who found, indeed, the facts to multiply
　With such rapidity of vice and woe,
That he had stripp'd off both his wings in quills,
And yet was in arrear of human ills.

4

His business so augmented of late years,
　That he was forced, against his will, no doubt,

(Just like those cherubs, earthly ministers)
   For some resource to turn himself about,
And claim the help of his celestial peers,
   To aid him ere he should be quite worn out
By the increased demand for his remarks;
Six angels and twelve saints were named his clerks.

5

This was a handsome board—at least for heaven;
   And yet they had even then enough to do,
So many conquerors' cars were daily driven,
   So many kingdoms fitted up anew;
Each day too slew its thousands six or seven,
   Till at the crowning carnage, Waterloo,
They threw their pens down in divine disgust—
The page was so besmear'd with blood and dust.

6

This by the way; 'tis not mine to record
   What angels shrink from: even the very devil
On this occasion his own work abhorr'd,
   So surfeited with the infernal revel;
Though he himself had sharpen'd every sword,
   It almost quench'd his innate thirst of evil.
(Here Satan's sole good work deserves insertion—
'Tis, that he has both generals in reversion.)

7

Let's skip a few short years of hollow peace,
   Which peopled earth no better, hell as wont,
And heaven none—they form the tyrant's lease
   With nothing but new names subscribed upon 't;
'Twill one day finish: meantime they increase,
   "With seven heads and ten horns," and all in front,
Like Saint John's foretold beast; but ours are born
Less formidable in the head than horn.

8

In the first year of freedom's second dawn
    Died George the Third; although no tyrant, one
Who shielded tyrants, till each sense withdrawn
    Left him nor mental nor external sun:
A better farmer ne'er brush'd dew from lawn,
    A weaker king never left a realm undone!
He died—but left his subjects still behind,
One half as mad—and t'other no less blind.

9

He died!—his death made no great stir on earth;
    His burial made some pomp; there was profusion
Of velvet, gilding, brass, and no great dearth
    Of aught but tears—save those shed by collusion;
For these things may be bought at their true worth:
    Of elegy there was the due infusion—
Bought also; and the torches, cloaks, and banners,
Heralds, and relics of old Gothic manners,

10

Form'd a sepulchral melo-drame. Of all
    The fools who flock'd to swell or see the show,
Who cared about the corpse? The funeral
    Made the attraction, and the black the woe.
There throbb'd not there a thought which pierced the pall;
    And when the gorgeous coffin was laid low,
It seem'd the mockery of hell to fold
The rottenness of eighty years in gold.

11

So mix his body with the dust! It might
    Return to what it *must* far sooner, were
The natural compound left alone to fight

Its way back into earth, and fire, and air;
But the unnatural balsams merely blight
What nature made him at his birth, as bare
As the mere million's base unmummied clay—
Yet all his spices but prolong decay.

12

He's dead—and upper earth with him has done:
He's buried; save the undertaker's bill,
Or lapidary scrawl, the world is gone
For him, unless he left a German will;
But where's the proctor who will ask his son?
In whom his qualities are reigning still,
Except that household virtue, most uncommon,
Of constancy to an unhandsome woman.

13

"God save the king!" It is a large economy
In God to save the like; but if he will
Be saving, all the better; for not one am I
Of those who think damnation better still:
I hardly know too if not quite alone am I
In this small hope of bettering future ill
By circumscribing, with some slight restriction,
The eternity of hell's hot jurisdiction.

14

I know this is unpopular; I know
'Tis blasphemous; I know one may be damn'd
For hoping no one else may e'er be so;
I know my catechism; I know we are cramm'd
With the best doctrines till we quite o'erflow;
I know that all save England's church have shamm'd,
And that the other twice two hundred churches
And synagogues have made a *damn'd* bad purchase.

15

God help us all! God help me too! I am,
    God knows, as helpless as the devil can wish,
And not a whit more difficult to damn
    Than is to bring to land a late-hook'd fish,
Or to the butcher to purvey the lamb;
    Not that I'm fit for such a noble dish
As one day will be that immortal fry
Of almost everybody born to die.

16

Saint Peter sat by the celestial gate,
    And nodded o'er his keys; when lo! there came
A wond'rous noise he had not heard of late—
    A rushing sound of wind, and stream, and flame;
In short, a roar of things extremely great,
    Which would have made aught save a saint exclaim;
But he, with first a start and then a wink,
Said, "There's another star gone out, I think!"

17

But ere he could return to his repose,
    A cherub flapp'd his right wing o'er his eyes—
At which Saint Peter yawn'd, and rubb'd his nose:
    "Saint porter," said the Angel, "prithee rise!"
Waving a goodly wing, which glow'd, as glows
    An earthly peacock's tail, with heavenly dyes;
To which the Saint replied, "Well, what's the matter?
Is Lucifer come back with all this clatter?"

18

"No," quoth the Cherub; "George the Third is dead."
    "And who *is* George the Third?" replied the Apostle;
"What George? what Third?" "The King of England," said

The Angel. "Well! he won't find kings to jostle
Him on his way; but does he wear his head?
    Because the last we saw here had a tussle,
And ne'er would have got into heaven's good graces,
Had he not flung his head in all our faces.

19

"He was, if I remember, king of France;
    That head of his, which could not keep a crown
On earth, yet ventured in my face to advance
    A claim to those of martyrs—like my own:
If I had had my sword, as I had once
    When I cut ears off, I had cut him down;
But having but my *keys,* and not my brand,
I only knock'd his head from out his hand.

20

"And then he set up such a headless howl,
    That all the saints came out, and took him in;
And there he sits by St. Paul, cheek by jowl;
    That fellow Paul—the parvenu! The skin
Of Saint Bartholomew, which makes his cowl
    In heaven, and upon earth redeem'd his sin
So as to make a martyr, never sped
Better than did this weak and wooden head.

21

"But had it come up here upon its shoulders,
    There would have been a different tale to tell:
The fellow feeling in the saint's beholders
    Seems to have acted on them like a spell,
And so this very foolish head heaven solders
    Back on its trunk: it may be very well,
And seems the custom here to overthrow
Whatever has been wisely done below."

22

The Angel answer'd, "Peter! do not pout;
   The king who comes has head and all entire,
And never knew much what it was about—
   He did as doth the puppet—by its wire,
And will be judged like all the rest, no doubt:
   My business and your own is not to inquire
Into such matters, but to mind our cue—
Which is to act as we are bid to do."

23

While thus they spake, the angelic caravan,
   Arriving like a rush of mighty wind,
Cleaving the fields of space, as doth the swan
   Some silver stream (say Ganges, Nile, or Inde,
Or Thames, or Tweed) and midst them an old man
   With an old soul, and both extremely blind,
Halted before the gate, and in his shroud
Seated their fellow traveler on a cloud.

24

But bringing up the rear of this bright host
   A Spirit of a different aspect waved
His wings, like thunderclouds above some coast
   Whose barren beach with frequent wrecks is paved;
His brow was like the deep when tempest-tossed;
   Fierce and unfathomable thoughts engraved
Eternal wrath on his immortal face,
And *where* he gazed a gloom pervaded space.

25

As he drew near, he gazed upon the gate
   Ne'er to be enter'd more by him or sin,
With such a glance of supernatural hate,

As made Saint Peter wish himself within;
He potter'd with his keys at a great rate,
  And sweated through his apostolic skin:
Of course his perspiration was but ichor,
Or some such other spiritual liquor.

26

The very cherubs huddled altogether,
  Like birds when soars the falcon; and they felt
A tingling to the tip of every feather,
  And form'd a circle like Orion's belt
Around their poor old charge; who scarce knew whither
  His guards had led him, though they gently dealt
With royal manes (for by many stories,
And true, we learn the angels all are Tories).

27

As things were in this posture, the gate flew
  Asunder, and the flashing of its hinges
Flung over space an universal hue
  Of many-colored flame, until its tinges
Reach'd even our speck of earth, and made a new
  Aurora borealis spread its fringes
O'er the North Pole; the same seen, when icebound,
By Captain Parry's crews, in "Melville's Sound."

28

And from the gate thrown open issued beaming
  A beautiful and mighty Thing of Light,
Radiant with glory, like a banner streaming
  Victorious from some world-o'erthrowing fight:
My poor comparisons must needs be teeming
  With earthly likenesses, for here the night
Of clay obscures our best conceptions, saving
Johanna Southcote, or Bob Southey raving.

29

'Twas the Archangel Michael: all men know
    The make of angels and archangels, since
There's scarce a scribbler has not one to show,
    From the fiends' leader to the angels' prince.
There also are some altar pieces, though
    I really can't say that they much evince
One's inner notions of immortal spirits;
But let the connoisseurs explain *their* merits.

30

Michael flew forth in glory and in good;
    A goodly work of him from whom all glory
And good arise; the portal past—he stood;
    Before him the young cherubs and saint hoary,
(I say *young*, begging to be understood
    By looks, not years; and should be very sorry
To state, they were not older than Saint Peter,
But merely that they seem'd a little sweeter).

31

The cherubs and the saints bow'd down before
    That arch-angelic Hierarch, the first
Of Essences angelical, who wore
    The aspect of a god; but this ne'er nursed
Pride in his heavenly bosom, in whose core
    No thought, save for his Maker's service, durst
Intrude, however glorified and high;
He knew him but the viceroy of the sky.

32

He and the somber silent Spirit met—
    They knew each other both for good and ill;
Such was their power, that neither could forget

His former friend and future foe; but still
There was a high, immortal, proud regret
    In either's eye, as if 'twere less their will
Than destiny to make the eternal years
Their date of war, and their "Champ Clos" the spheres.

33

But here they were in neutral space: we know
    From Job, that Satan hath the power to pay
A heavenly visit thrice a year or so;
    And that "the Sons of God," like those of clay,
Must keep him company; and we might show,
    From the same book, in how polite a way
The dialogue is held between the Powers
Of Good and Evil—but 'twould take up hours.

34

And this is not a theologic tract,
    To prove with Hebrew and with Arabic
If Job be allegory or a fact,
    But a true narrative; and thus I pick
From out the whole but such and such an act
    As sets aside the slightest thought of trick.
'Tis every tittle true, beyond suspicion,
And accurate as any other vision.

35

The spirits were in neutral space, before
    The gate of heaven; like eastern thresholds is
The place where Death's grand cause is argued o'er,
    And souls dispatched to that world or to this;
And therefore Michael and the other wore
    A civil aspect: though they did not kiss,
Yet still between his Darkness and his Brightness
There passed a mutual glance of great politeness.

36

The Archangel bowed, not like a modern beau,
    But with a graceful Oriental bend,
Pressing one radiant arm just where below
    The heart in good men is supposed to tend.
He turned as to an equal, not too low,
    But kindly; Satan met his ancient friend
With more hauteur, as might an old Castilian
Poor noble meet a mushroom rich civilian.

37

He merely bent his diabolic brow
    An instant; and then raising it, he stood
In act to assert his right or wrong, and show
    Cause why King George by no means could or should
Make out a case to be exempt from woe
    Eternal, more than other kings endued
With better sense and hearts, whom history mentions,
Who long have "paved hell with their good intentions."

38

Michael began: "What wouldst thou with this man,
    Now dead, and brought before the Lord? What ill
Hath he wrought since his mortal race began,
    That thou can'st claim him: Speak! and do thy will,
If it be just: if in this earthly span
    He hath been greatly failing to fulfill
His duties as a king and mortal, say,
And he is thine; if not, let him have way."

39

"Michael!" replied the Prince of Air, "even here,
    Before the gate of him thou servest, must
I claim my subject; and will make appear

That as he was my worshipper in dust,
So shall he be in spirit, although dear
To thee and thine, because nor wine nor lust
Were of his weaknesses; yet on the throne
He reign'd o'er millions to serve me alone.

40

"Look to *our* earth, or rather *mine;* it was,
    Once, more thy master's but I triumph not
In this poor planet's conquest, nor, alas!
    Need he thou servest envy me my lot:
With all the myriads of bright worlds which pass
    In worship round him, he may have forgot
Yon weak creation of such paltry things;
I think few worth damnation save their kings,

41

"And these but as a kind of quit-rent, to
    Assert my right as lord; and even had
I such an inclination, 'twere (as you
    Well know) superfluous; they are grown so bad,
That hell has nothing better left to do
    Than leave them to themselves: so much more mad
And evil by their own internal curse,
Heaven cannot make them better, nor I worse.

42

"Look to the earth, I said, and say again:
    When this old, blind, mad, helpless, weak, poor worm,
Began in youth's first bloom and flush to reign,
    The world and he both wore a different form,
And much of earth and all the watery plain
    Of ocean call'd him king: through many a storm
His isles had floated on the abyss of Time;
For the rough virtues chose them for their clime.

43

"He came to his scepter, young; he leaves it, old:
    Look to the state in which he found his realm,
And left it; and his annals too behold,
    How to a minion first he gave the helm;
How grew upon his heart a thirst for gold,
    The beggar's vice, which can but overwhelm
The meanest hearts; and for the rest, but glance
Thine eye along America and France!

44

"'Tis true, he was a tool from first to last
    (I have the workmen safe); but as a tool
So let him be consumed! From out the past
    Of ages, since mankind have known the rule
Of monarchs—from the bloody rolls amass'd
    Of sin and slaughter—from the Caesar's school,
Take the worst pupil; and produce a reign
More drench'd with gore, more cumber'd with the slain!

45

"He ever warr'd with freedom and the free:
    Nations as men, home subjects, foreign foes,
So that they utter'd the word 'Liberty!'
    Found George the Third their first opponent. Whose
History was ever stain'd as his will be
    With national and individual woes?
I grant his household abstinence; I grant
His neutral virtues, which most monarchs want;

46

"I know he was a constant consort; own
    He was a decent sire, and middling lord.
All this is much, and most upon a throne;

As temperance, if at Apicius' board,
Is more than at an anchorite's supper shown.
   I grant him all the kindest can accord;
And this was well for him, but not for those
Millions who found him what oppression chose.

47

"The new world shook him off; the old yet groans
   Beneath what he and his prepared, if not
Completed: he leaves heirs on many thrones
   To all his vices, without what begot
Compassion for him—his tame virtues; drones
   Who sleep, or despots who have now forgot
A lesson which shall be retaught them, wake
Upon the throne of Earth; but let them quake!

48

"Five millions of the primitive, who hold
   The faith which makes ye great on earth, implored
A *part* of that vast *all* they held of old—
   Freedom to worship—not alone your Lord,
Michael, but you, and you, Saint Peter! Cold
   Must be your souls, if you have not abhorr'd
The foe to Catholic participation
In all the license of a Christian nation.

49

"True! he allow'd them to pray God; but as
   A consequence of prayer, refused the law
Which would have placed them upon the same base
   With those who did not hold the saints in awe."
But here Saint Peter started from his place,
   And cried, "You may the prisoner withdraw:
Ere Heaven shall ope her portals to this Guelf,
While I am guard, may I be damn'd myself!

50

"Sooner will I with Cerberus exchange
  My office (and *his* is no sinecure)
Than see this royal Bedlam bigot range
  The azure fields of heaven, of that be sure!"
"Saint!" replied Satan, "you do well to avenge
  The wrongs he made your satellites endure;
And if to this exchange you should be given,
I'll try to coax *our* Cerberus up to heaven."

51

Here Michael interposed: "Good saint! and devil!
  Pray not so fast; you both outrun discretion.
Saint Peter! you were wont to be more civil:
  Satan! excuse this warmth of his expression,
And condescension to the vulgar's level:
  Even saints sometimes forget themselves in session.
Have you got more to say?"—"No!"—"If you please,
I'll trouble you to call your witnesses."

52

Then Satan turn'd and wav'd his swarthy hand,
  Which stirr'd with its electric qualities
Clouds farther off than we can understand,
  Although we find him sometimes in our skies;
Infernal thunder shook both sea and land
  In all the planets, and hell's batteries
Let off the artillery, which Milton mentions
As one of Satan's most sublime inventions.

53

This was a signal unto such damn'd souls
  As have the privilege of their damnation
Extended far beyond the mere controls

Of worlds past, present, or to come; no station
Is theirs particularly in the rolls
Of hell assigned; but where their inclination
Or business carries them in search of game,
They may range freely—being damn'd the same.

54

They are proud of this—as very well they may,
    It being a sort of knighthood, or gilt key
Stuck in their loins; or like to an "entré"
    Up the back stairs, or such freemasonry:
I borrow my comparisons from clay,
    Being clay myself. Let not those spirits be
Offended with such base low likenesses;
We know their posts are nobler far than these.

55

When the great signal ran from heaven to hell—
    About ten million times the distance reckon'd
From our sun to its earth, as we can tell
    How much time it takes up, even to a second,
For every ray that travels to dispel
    The fogs of London; through which, dimly beacon'd,
The weathercocks are gilt, some thrice a year,
If that the *summer* is not too severe—

56

I say that I can tell—'twas half a minute;
    I know the solar beams take up more time
Ere, pack'd up for their journey, they begin it;
    But then their telegraph is less sublime,
And if they ran a race, they would not win it
    'Gainst Satan's couriers bound for their own clime.
The sun takes up some years for every ray
To reach its goal—the devil not half a day.

57

Upon the verge of space, about the size
  Of half-a-crown, a little speck appear'd,
(I've seen a something like it in the skies
  In the Aegean, ere a squall); it near'd,
And, growing bigger, took another guise;
  Like an aerial ship it tack'd, and steer'd
Or *was* steer'd (I am doubtful of the grammar
Of the last phrase, which makes the stanza stammer—

58

But take your choice); and then it grew a cloud,
  And so it was—a cloud of witnesses.
But such a cloud! No land ere saw a crowd
  Of locusts numerous as the heavens saw these;
They shadow'd with their myriads space; their loud
  And varied cries were like those of wild geese,
(If nations may be liken'd to a goose)
And realized the phrase of "hell broke loose."

59

Here crash'd a sturdy oath of stout John Bull,
  Who damn'd away his eyes as heretofore:
There Paddy brogued "by Jasus!"—"What's your wull?"
  The temperate Scot exclaim'd: the French ghost swore
In certain terms I shan't translate in full,
  As the first coachman will; and midst the roar
The voice of Jonathan was heard to express,
"*Our* President is going to war, I guess."

60

Besides there were the Spaniard, Dutch, and Dane;
  In short, an universal shoal of shades
From Otaheite's Isle to Salisbury Plain,

Of all climes and professions, years and trades,
Ready to swear against the good king's reign,
    Bitter as clubs in cards are against spades:
All summon'd by this grand "subpoena," to
Try if kings mayn't be damn'd, like me or you.

61

When Michael saw this host, he first grew pale,
    As angels can; next, like Italian twilight,
He turned all colors—as a peacock's tail,
    Or sunset streaming through a Gothic skylight
In some old abbey, or a trout not stale,
    Or distant lightning on the horizon *by* night,
Or a fresh rainbow, or a grand review
Of thirty regiments in red, green, and blue.

62

Then he address'd himself to Satan: "Why—
    My good old friend, for such I deem you, though
Our different parties make us fight so shy,
    I ne'er mistake you for a *personal* foe;
Our difference is *political,* and I
    Trust that, whatever may occur below,
You know my great respect for you; and this
Makes me regret whate'er you do amiss—

63

"Why, my dear Lucifer, would you abuse
    My call for witnesses? I did not mean
That you should half of earth and hell produce;
    'Tis even superfluous, since two honest, clean,
True testimonies are enough: we lose
    Our time, nay, our eternity, between
The accusation and defense: if we
Hear both, 'twill stretch our immortality."

— 166 —

64

Satan replied, "To me the matter is
   Indifferent, in a personal point of view:
I can have fifty better souls than this
   With far less trouble than we have gone through
Already; and I merely argued his
   Late Majesty of Britain's case with you
Upon a point of form: you may dispose
Of him; I've kings enough below, God knows!"

Thus spoke the Demon (late call'd "multifaced"
   By multo-scribbling Southey). "Then we'll call
One or two persons of the myriads placed
   Around our congress, and dispense with all
The rest," quoth Michael: "Who may be so graced
   As to speak first? there's choice enough—who shall
It be?" Then Satan answered, "There are many;
But you may choose Jack Wilkes as well as any."

66

A merry, cock-eyed, curious looking Sprite,
   Upon the instant started from the throng,
Dressed in a fashion now forgotten quite;
   For all the fashions of the flesh stick long
By people in the next world; where unite
   All the costumes since Adam's, right or wrong,
From Eve's fig-leaf down to the petticoat,
Almost as scanty, of days less remote.

The Spirit look'd around upon the crowds
   Assembled, and exclaim'd, "My friends of all
The spheres, we shall catch cold amongst these clouds;

So let's to business: why this general call?
If those are freeholders I see in shrouds,
    And 'tis for an election that they bawl,
Behold a candidate with unturn'd-coat!
Saint Peter, may I count upon your vote?"

68

"Sir," replied Michael, "you mistake: these things
    Are of a former life, and what we do
Above is more august; to judge of kings
    Is the tribunal met; so now you know."
"Then I presume those gentlemen with wings,"
    Said Wilkes, "are cherubs; and that soul below
Looks much like George the Third; but to my mind
A good deal older—Bless me! is he blind?"

69

"He is what you behold him, and his doom
    Depends upon his deeds," the Angel said.
"If you have ought to arraign in him, the tomb
    Gives license to the humblest beggar's head
To lift itself against the loftiest."—"Some,"
    Said Wilkes, "don't wait to see them laid in lead,
For such a liberty—and I, for one,
Have told them what I thought beneath the sun."

71

"*Above* the sun repeat, then, what thou hast
    To urge against him," said the Archangel. "Why,"
Replied the Spirit, "since old scores are past,
    Must I turn evidence? In faith, not I.
Besides, I beat him hollow at the last,
    With all his Lords and Commons: in the sky
I don't like ripping up old stories, since
His conduct was but natural in a prince.

71

"Foolish, no doubt, and wicked, to oppress
A poor unlucky devil without a shilling;
But then I blame the man himself much less
    Than Bute and Grafton, and shall be unwilling
To see him punish'd here for their excess,
    Since they were both damn'd long ago, and still in
Their place below; for me, I have forgiven,
And vote his 'habeas corpus' into heaven."

72

"Wilkes," said the Devil, "I understand all this;
    You turn'd to half a courtier ere you died,
And seem to think it would not be amiss
    To grow a whole one on the other side
Of Charon's ferry; you forget that *his*
    Reign is concluded; whatsoe'er betide,
He won't be sovereign more: you've lost your labor
For at the best he will but be your neighbor.

73

"However, I knew what to think of it,
    When I beheld you in your jesting way
Flitting and whispering round about the spit
    Where Belial, upon duty for the day,
With Fox's lard was basting William Pitt,
    His pupil; I knew what to think, I say:
That fellow even in hell breeds farther ills;
I'll have him *gagg'd*—'twas one of his own bills.

74

"Call Junius!" From the crowd a Shadow stalk'd,
    And at the name there was a general squeeze,
So that the very ghosts no longer walk'd

In comfort, at their own aerial ease,
But were all ramm'd, and jamm'd (but to be balk'd,
    As we shall see) and jostled hands and knees,
Like wind compress'd and pent within a bladder,
Or like a human cholic, which is sadder.

75

The Shadow came! a tall, thin, gray-hair'd figure,
    That look'd as it had been a shade on earth;
Quick in its motions, with an air of vigor,
    But naught to mark its breeding or its birth:
Now it wax'd little, then again grew bigger,
    With now an air of gloom, or savage mirth;
But as you gazed upon its features, they
Changed every instant—to *what*, none could stay.

76

The more intently the ghosts gazed, the less
    Could they distinguish whose the features were;
The Devil himself seem'd puzzled even to guess;
    They varied like a dream—now here, now there;
And several people swore from out the press,
    They knew him perfectly; and one could swear
He was his father; upon which another
Was sure he was his mother's cousin's brother:

77

Another, that he was a duke, or knight,
    An orator, a lawyer, or a priest,
A nabob, a man-midwife; but the wight
    Mysterious changed his countenance at least
As oft as they their minds: though in full sight
    He stood, the puzzle only was increased;
The man was a phantasmagoria in
Himself—he was so volatile and thin!

78

The moment that you had pronounced him *one*,
　　Presto! his face changed, and he was another;
And when that change was hardly well put on,
　　It varied, till I don't think his own mother
(If that he had a mother) would her son
　　Have known, he shifted so from one to t'other,
Till guessing from a pleasure grew a task,
At this epistolary "iron mask."

79

For sometimes he like Cerberus would seem—
　　"Three gentlemen at once," (as sagely says
Good Mrs. Malaprop); then you might deem
　　That he was not even *one;* now many rays
Were flashing round him; and now a thick steam
　　Hid him from sight—like fogs on London days:
Now Burke, now Tooke, he grew to people's fancies,
And *certes* often like Sir Philip Francis.

80

I've an hypothesis—'tis quite my own;
　　I never let it out till now, for fear
Of doing people harm about the throne,
　　And injuring some minister or peer
On whom the stigma might perhaps be blown;
　　It is—my gentle public, lend thine ear!
'Tis, that what Junius we are wont to call,
Was *really, truly,* nobody at all.

81

I don't see wherefore letters should not be
　　Written without hands, since we daily view
Them written without heads; and books we see

Are fill'd as well without the latter too:
And really till we fix on somebody
    For certain sure to claim them as his due,
Their author, like the Niger's mouth, will bother
The world to say if *there* be mouth or author.

82

"And who and what art thou?" the Archangel said.
    "For *that*, you may consult my title page,"
Replied this mighty Shadow of a Shade:
    "If I have kept my secret half an age,
I scarce shall tell it now."—"Canst thou upbraid,"
    Continued Michael, "George Rex, or allege
Aught further?" Junius answer'd, "You had better
First ask him for *his* answer to my letter:

83

"My charges upon record will outlast
    The brass of both his epitaph and tomb."
"Repent'st thou not," said Michael, "of some past
    Exaggeration? something which may doom
Thyself, if false, as him if true? Thou wast
    Too bitter—is it not so? in thy gloom
Of passion?" "Passion!" cried the Phantom dim,
"I loved my country, and I hated him.

84

"What I have written, I have written: let
    The rest be on his head or mind" So spoke
Old 'Nominis Umbra'; and while speaking yet,
    Away he melted in celestial smoke.
Then Satan said to Michael, "Don't forget
    To call George Washington, and John Horne Tooke,
And Franklin"—but at this time there was heard
A cry for room, though not a phantom stirr'd.

At length with jostling, elbowing, and the aid
   Of cherubim appointed to that post,
The devil Asmodeus to the circle made
   His way, and look'd as if his journey cost
Some trouble. When his burden down he laid,
   "What's this?" cried Michael; "why, 'tis not a ghost?"
"I know it," quoth the incubus; "but he
Shall be one, if you leave the affair to me.

86

"Confound the Renegado! I have sprain'd
   My left wing, he's so heavy; one would think
Some of his works about his neck were chain'd.
   But to the point: while hovering o'er the brink
Of Skiddaw (where as usual it still rain'd),
   I saw a taper, far below me, wink,
And stooping, caught this fellow at a libel—
No less on History than the Holy Bible.

87

"The former is the devil's scripture, and
   The latter yours, good Michael; so the affair
Belongs to all of us, you understand.
   I snatch'd him up just as you see him there,
And brought him off for sentence out of hand:
   I've scarcely been ten minutes in the air—
At least a quarter it can hardly be:
I dare say that his wife is still at tea."

88

Here Satan said, "I know this man of old,
   And have expected him for some time here;
A sillier fellow you will scarce behold,

Or more conceited in his petty sphere:
But surely it was not worthwhile to fold
    Such trash below your wing, Asmodeus dear!
We had the poor wretch safe (without being bored
With carriage) coming of his own accord.

89

"But since he's here, let's see what he has done."
    "Done!" cried Asmodeus, "he anticipates
The very business you are now upon,
    And scribbles as if head clerk to the Fates.
Who knows to what his ribaldry may run,
    When such an ass as this, like Balaam's, prates?"
"Let's hear," quoth Michael, "what he has to say;
You know we're bound to that in every way."

90

Now the Bard, glad to get an audience, which
    By no means often was his case below,
Began to cough, and hawk, and hem, and pitch
    His voice into that awful note of woe
To all unhappy hearers within reach
    Of poets when the tide of rhyme's in flow;
But stuck fast with his first hexameter,
Not one of all whose gouty feet would stir.

91

But ere the spavin'd dactyls could be spurr'd
    Into recitative, in great dismay
Both cherubim and seraphim were heard
    To murmur loudly through their long array;
And Michael rose ere he could get a word
    Of all his founder'd verses under way,
And cried, "For God's sake stop, my friend! 'twere best—
'Non Di, non homines—' you know the rest."

92

A general bustle spread throughout the throng,
   Which seem'd to hold all verse in detestation;
The angels had of course enough of song
   When upon service; and the generation
Of ghosts had heard too much in life, not long
   Before, to profit by a new occasion;
The Monarch, mute till then, exclaim'd, "What! what!
Pye come again? No more—no more of that!"

93

The tumult grew, an universal cough
   Convulsed the skies, as during a debate,
When Castlereagh has been up long enough,
   (Before he was first minister of state,
I mean—the *slaves hear now*); some cried "off, off,"
   As at a farce; till grown quite desperate,
The Bard Saint Peter pray'd to interpose
(Himself an author) only for his prose.

94

The varlet was not an ill-favor'd knave;
   A good deal like a vulture in the face,
With a hook nose and a hawk's eye, which gave
   A smart and sharper looking sort of grace
To his whole aspect, which, though rather grave,
   Was by no means so ugly as his case;
But that indeed was hopeless as can be,
Quite a poetic felony *"de se."*

95

Then Michael blew his trump, and still'd the noise
   With one still greater, as is yet the mode
On earth besides; except some grumbling voice,

Which now and then will make a slight inroad
Upon decorous silence, few will twice
     Lift up their lungs when fairly overcrow'd;
And now the Bard could plead his own bad cause,
With all the attitudes of self-applause.

96

He said—(I only give the heads)—he said,
     He meant no harm in scribbling; 'twas his way
Upon all topics; 'twas, besides, his bread,
     Of which he butter'd both sides; 'twould delay
Too long the assembly (he was pleased to dread)
     And take up rather more time than a day,
To name his works—he would but cite a few—
Wat Tyler—Rhymes on Blenheim—Waterloo.

97

He had written praises of a regicide;
     He had written praises of all kings whatever;
He had written for republics far and wide,
     And then against them bitterer than ever;
For pantisocracy he once had cried
     Aloud, a scheme less moral than 'twas clever;
Then grew a hearty anti-jacobin—
Had turn'd his coat—and would have turn'd his skin.

98

He had sung against all battles, and again
     In their high praise and glory: he had call'd
Reviewing "the ungentle craft," and then
     Become as base a critic as ere crawl'd—
Fed, paid, and pamper'd by the very men
     By whom his muse and morals had been maul'd:
He had written much blank verse, and blanker prose,
And more of both than anybody knows.

99

He had written Wesley's life—here, turning round
　　To Satan, "Sir, I'm ready to write yours,
In two octavo volumes, nicely bound,
　　With notes and preface, all that most allures
The pious purchaser; and there's no ground
　　For fear, for I can choose my own reviewers:
So let me have the proper documents,
That I may add you to my other saints."

100

Satan bow'd, and was silent. "Well, if you,
　　With amiable modesty, decline
My offer, what says Michael? There are few
　　Whose memoirs could be render'd more divine.
Mine is a pen of all work; not so new
　　As it was once, but I would make you shine
Like your own trumpet; by the way, my own
Has more of brass in it, and is as well blown.

101

"But talking about trumpets, here's my Vision!
　　Now you shall judge, all people; yes, you shall
Judge with my judgment! and by my decision
　　Be guided who shall enter heaven or fall!
I settle all these things by intuition,
　　Times present, past, to come, heaven, hell, and all,
Like King Alfonso! When I thus see double,
I save the Deity some worlds of trouble."

102

He ceased; and drew forth an MS; and no
　　Persuasion on the part of devils, or saints,
Or angels, now could stop the torrent; so

He read the first three lines of the contents;
But at the fourth, the whole spiritual show
Had vanish'd, with variety of scents,
Ambrosial and sulphureous, as they sprang,
Like lightning, off from his "melodious twang."

103

Those grand heroics acted as a spell:
The angels stopp'd their ears and plied their pinions;
The devils ran howling, deafen'd, down to hell;
The ghosts fled, gibbering, for their own dominions—
(For 'tis not yet decided where they dwell,
And I leave every man to his opinions);
Michael took refuge in his trump—but lo!
His teeth were set on edge, he could not blow!

104

Saint Peter, who has hitherto been known
For an impetuous saint, upraised his keys,
And at the fifth line knock'd the Poet down;
Who fell like Phaeton, but more at ease,
Into his lake, for there he did not drown,
A different web being by the Destinies
Woven for the Laureate's final wreath, whene'er
Reform shall happen either here or there.

105

He first sunk to the bottom—like his works,
But soon rose to the surface—like himself;
For all corrupted things are buoy'd, like corks,
By their own rottenness, light as an elf,
Or wisp that flits o'er a morass: he lurks,
It may be, still, like dull books on a shelf,
In his own den, to scrawl some "Life" or "Vision,"
As Wellborn says—"the devil turn'd precisian."

106

As for the rest, to come to the conclusion
Of this true dream, the telescope is gone
Which kept my optics free from all delusion,
     And show'd me what I in my turn have shown:
All I saw farther in the last confusion,
     Was, that King George slipp'd into heaven for one;
And when the tumult dwindled to a calm,
I left him practicing the hundredth psalm.

From

Don Juan

From CANTO I

1

I want a hero: an uncommon want,
    When every year and month sends forth a new one,
Till, after cloying the gazettes with cant,
    The age discovers he is not the true one;
Of such as these I should not care to vaunt,
    I'll therefore take our ancient friend Don Juan,
We all have seen him in the pantomime
Sent to the devil, somewhat ere his time.

5

Brave men were living before Agamemnon
    And since, exceeding valorous and sage,
A good deal like him too, though quite the same
        none;
    But then they shone not on the poet's page,
And so have been forgotten—I condemn none,
    But can't find any in the present age
Fit for my poem (that is, for my new one);
So, as I said, I'll take my friend Don Juan.

6

Most epic poets plunge in "medias res,"
    (Horace makes this the heroic turnpike road)
And then your hero tells, whene'er you please,
    What went before—by way of episode,
While seated after dinner at his ease,
    Beside his mistress in some soft abode,
Palace, or garden, paradise, or cavern,
Which serves the happy couple for a tavern.

7

That is the usual method, but not mine—
  My way is to begin with the beginning;
The regularity of my design
  Forbids all wandering as the worst of sinning,
And therefore I shall open with a line
  (Although it cost me half an hour in spinning)
Narrating somewhat of Don Juan's father,
And also of his mother, if you'd rather.

8

In Seville was he born, a pleasant city,
  Famous for oranges and women—he
Who has not seen it will be much to pity,
  So says the proverb—and I quite agree;
Of all the Spanish towns is none more pretty,
  Cadiz perhaps—but that you soon may see—
Don Juan's parents lived beside the river,
A noble stream, and call'd the Guadalquivir.

9

His father's name was Jóse—*Don,* of course,
  A true Hidalgo, free from every stain
Of Moor or Hebrew blood, he traced his source
  Through the most Gothic gentlemen of Spain;
A better cavalier ne'er mounted horse,
  Or, being mounted, e'er got down again,
Than Jóse, who begot our hero, who
Begot—but that's to come——Well, to renew:

10

His mother was a learned lady, famed
  For every branch of every science known—
In every Christian language ever named,
  With virtues equall'd by her wit alone,

She made the cleverest people quite ashamed,
   And even the good with inward envy groan,
Finding themselves so very much exceeded
In their own way by all the things that she did.

11

Her memory was a mine: she knew by heart
   All Calderon and greater part of Lopé,
So that if any actor miss'd his part
   She could have served him for the prompter's copy;
For her Feinagle's were an useless art,
   And he himself obliged to shut up shop—he
Could never make a memory so fine as
That which adorn'd the brain of Donna Inez.

12

Her favorite science was the mathematical,
   Her noblest virtue was her magnanimity,
Her wit (she sometimes tried at wit) was Attic all,
   Her serious sayings darken'd to sublimity;
In short, in all things she was fairly what I call
   A prodigy—her morning dress was dimity,
Her evening silk, or, in the summer, muslin,
And other stuffs, with which I won't stay puzzling.

13

She knew the Latin—that is, "the Lord's prayer,"
   And Greek—the alphabet—I'm nearly sure;
She read some French romances here and there,
   Although her mode of speaking was not pure;
For native Spanish she had no great care,
   At least her conversation was obscure;
Her thoughts were theorems, her words a problem,
As if she deem'd that mystery would ennoble 'em.

22

'Tis pity learned virgins ever wed
With persons of no sort of education,
Or gentlemen, who, though well-born and bred,
Grow tired of scientific conversation:
I don't choose to say much upon this head,
    I'm a plain man, and in a single station,
But—Oh! ye lords of ladies intellectual,
Inform us truly, have they not hen-peck'd you all?

23

Don Jóse and his lady quarrel'd—*why,*
    Not any of the many could divine,
Though several thousand people chose to try,
    'Twas surely no concern of theirs nor mine;
I loathe that low vice curiosity,
    But if there's any thing in which I shine
'Tis in arranging all my friends' affairs
Not having, of my own, domestic cares.

24

And so I interfered, and with the best
    Intentions, but their treatment was not kind;
I think the foolish people were possess'd,
    For neither of them could I ever find,
Although their porter afterwards confess'd—
    But that's no matter, and the worst's behind,
For little Juan o'er me threw, down stairs,
A pail of housemaid's water unawares.

25

A little curly-headed, good-for-nothing,
    And mischief-making monkey from his birth;
His parents ne'er agreed except in doting
    Upon the most unquiet imp on earth;

Instead of quarreling, had they been but both in
   Their senses, they'd have sent young master forth
To school, or had him soundly whipp'd at home,
   To teach him manners for the time to come.

26

Don Jóse and the Donna Inez led
   For some time an unhappy sort of life,
Wishing each other, not divorced, but dead;
   They lived respectably as man and wife,
Their conduct was exceedingly well-bred,
   And gave no outward signs of inward strife,
Until at length the smother'd fire broke out,
And put the business past all kind of doubt.

27

For Inez call'd some druggists and physicians,
   And tried to prove her loving lord was *mad*,
But as he had some lucid intermissions,
   She next decided he was only *bad*;
Yet when they ask'd her for her depositions,
   No sort of explanation could be had,
Save that her duty both to man and God
Required this conduct—which seem'd very odd.

28

She kept a journal, where his faults were noted,
   And open'd certain trunks of books and letters,
All which might, if occasion served, be quoted;
   And then she had all Seville for abettors,
Besides her good old grandmother (who doted);
   The hearers of her case became repeaters,
Then advocates, inquisitors, and judges,
Some for amusement, others for old grudges.

29

And then this best and meekest woman bore
    With such serenity her husband's woes,
Just as the Spartan ladies did of yore,
    Who saw their spouses kill'd, and nobly chose
Never to say a word about them more—
    Calmly she heard each calumny that rose,
And saw *his* agonies with such sublimity,
That all the world exclaim'd, "What magnanimity!"

30

No doubt, this patience, when the world is damning us,
    Is philosophic in our former friends;
'Tis also pleasant to be deem'd magnanimous,
    The more so in obtaining our own ends;
And what the lawyers call a *"malus animus,"*
    Conduct like this by no means comprehends:
Revenge in person's certainly no virtue,
But then 'tis not *my* fault, if *others* hurt you.

31

And if our quarrels should rip up old stories,
    And help them with a lie or two additional,
I'm not to blame, as you well know, no more is
    Anyone else—they were become traditional;
Besides, their resurrection aids our glories
    By contrast, which is what we just were wishing all:
And science profits by this resurrection—
Dead scandals form good subjects for dissection.

32

Their friends had tried at reconciliation,
    Then their relations, who made matters worse;
('Twere hard to say upon a like occasion
    To whom it may be best to have recourse—

I can't say much for friend or yet relation):
The lawyers did their utmost for divorce,
But scarce a fee was paid on either side
Before, unluckily, Don Jóse died.

33

He died: and most unluckily, because,
  According to all hints I could collect
From counsel learned in those kinds of laws,
  (Although their talk's obscure and circumspect)
His death contrived to spoil a charming cause;
  A thousand pities also with respect
To public feeling, which on this occasion
Was manifested in a great sensation.

37

Dying intestate, Juan was sole heir
  To a chancery suit, and messuages, and lands,
Which, with a long minority and care,
  Promised to turn out well in proper hands:
Inez became sole guardian, which was fair,
  And answer'd but to nature's just demands;
An only son left with an only mother
Is brought up much more wisely than another.

38

Sagest of women, even of widows, she
  Resolved that Juan should be quite a paragon,
And worthy of the noblest pedigree:
  (His sire was of Castile, his dam from Arragon).
Then for accomplishments of chivalry,
  In case our lord the king should go to war again,
He learn'd the arts of riding, fencing, gunnery,
And how to scale a fortress—or a nunnery.

39

But that which Donna Inez most desired,
And saw into herself each day before all
The learned tutors whom for him she hired,
    Was that his breeding should be strictly moral;
Much into all his studies she inquired,
    And so they were submitted first to her, all,
Arts, sciences, no branch was made a mystery
To Juan's eyes, excepting natural history.

40

The languages, especially the dead,
    The sciences, and most of all the abstruse,
The arts, at least all such as could be said
    To be the most remote from common use,
In all these he was much and deeply read;
    But not a page of anything that's loose,
Or hints continuation of the species,
Was ever suffer'd, lest he should grow vicious.

41

His classic studies made a little puzzle,
    Because of filthy loves of gods and goddesses,
Who in the earlier ages made a bustle,
    But never put on pantaloons or bodices;
His reverend tutors had at times a tussle,
    And for their *Aeneids, Iliads,* and *Odysseys,*
Were forced to make an odd sort of apology,
For Donna Inez dreaded the mythology.

42

Ovid's a rake, as half his verses show him,
    Anacreon's morals are a still worse sample,
Catullus scarcely has a decent poem,
    I don't think Sappho's *Ode* a good example,

Although Longinus tells us there is no hymn
    Where the sublime soars forth on wings more ample;
But Virgil's songs are pure, except that horrid one
    Beginning with *"Formosum Pastor Corydon."*

43

Lucretius' irreligion is too strong
    For early stomachs, to prove wholesome food;
I can't help thinking Juvenal was wrong,
    Although no doubt his real intent was good,
For speaking out so plainly in his song,
    So much indeed as to be downright rude;
And then what proper person can be partial
To all those nauseous epigrams of Martial?

44

Juan was taught from out the best edition,
    Expurgated by learned men, who place,
Judiciously, from out the schoolboy's vision,
    The grosser parts; but fearful to deface
Too much their modest bard by this omission,
    And pitying sore his mutilated case,
They only add them all in an appendix,
Which saves, in fact, the trouble of an index;

52

For my part I say nothing—nothing—but
    This I will say—my reasons are my own—
That if I had an only son to put
    To school (as God be praised that I have none)
'Tis not with Donna Inez I would shut
    Him up to learn his catechism alone,
No—no—I'd send him out betimes to college,
For there it was I pick'd up my own knowledge.

53

For there one learns—'tis not for me to boast,
  Though I acquired—but I pass over *that*,
As well as all the Greek I since have lost:
  I say that there's the place—but *"Verbum sat,"*
I think I pick'd up too, as well as most,
  Knowledge of matters—but no matter *what*—
I never married—but, I think, I know
That sons should not be educated so.

54

Young Juan now was sixteen years of age,
  Tall, handsome, slender, but well knit; he seem'd
Active, though not so sprightly, as a page;
  And everybody but his mother deem'd
Him almost man; but she flew in a rage,
  And bit her lips (for else she might have scream'd),
If any said so, for to be precocious
Was in her eyes a thing the most atrocious.

55

Amongst her numerous acquaintance, all
  Selected for discretion and devotion,
There was the Donna Julia, whom to call
  Pretty were but to give a feeble notion
Of many charms in her as natural
  As sweetness to the flower, or salt to ocean,
Her zone to Venus, or his bow to Cupid,
(But this last simile is trite and stupid).

56

The darkness of her oriental eye
  Accorded with her Moorish origin;
(Her blood was not all Spanish, by the by:
  In Spain, you know, this is a sort of sin).

When proud Granada fell, and, forced to fly,
　Boabdil wept, of Donna Julia's kin
Some went to Africa, some stayed in Spain,
　Her great great grandmamma chose to remain.

57

She married (I forget the pedigree)
　With an Hidalgo, who transmitted down
His blood less noble than such blood should be;
　At such alliances his sires would frown,
In that point so precise in each degree
That they bred *in and in*, as might be shown,
Marrying their cousins—nay, their aunts, and nieces,
Which always spoils the breed, if it increases.

58

This heathenish cross restored the breed again,
　Ruin'd its blood, but much improved its flesh;
For, from a root the ugliest in Old Spain
　Sprung up a branch as beautiful as fresh;
The sons no more were short, the daughters plain:
　But there's a rumor which I fain would hush,
'Tis said that Donna Julia's grandmamma
Produced her Don more heirs at love than law.

59

However this might be, the race went on
　Improving still through every generation,
Until it center'd in an only son,
　Who left an only daughter; my narration
May have suggested that this single one
　Could be but Julia (whom on this occasion
I shall have much to speak about), and she
Was married, charming, chaste, and twenty-three.

60

Her eye (I'm very fond of handsome eyes)
 Was large and dark, suppressing half its fire
Until she spoke, then through its soft disguise
 Flash'd an expression more of pride than ire,
And love than either; and there would arise
 A something in them which was not desire,
But would have been, perhaps, but for the soul
Which struggled through and chasten'd down the whole.

61

Her glossy hair was cluster'd o'er a brow
 Bright with intelligence, and fair and smooth;
Her eyebrow's shape was like the aerial bow,
 Her cheek all purple with the beam of youth,
Mounting, at times, to a transparent glow,
 As if her veins ran lightning; she, in sooth,
Possess'd an air and grace by no means common:
Her stature tall—I hate a dumpy woman.

62

Wedded she was some years, and to a man
 Of fifty, and such husbands are in plenty;
And yet, I think, instead of such a ONE
 'Twere better to have TWO of five and twenty,
Especially in countries near the sun:
 And now I think on't, *"mi vien in mente,"*
Ladies even of the most uneasy virtue
Prefer a spouse whose age is short of thirty.

63

'Tis a sad thing, I cannot choose but say,
 And all the fault of that indecent sun,
Who cannot leave alone our helpless clay,
 But will keep baking, broiling, burning on,

That howsoever people fast and pray
  The flesh is frail, and so the soul undone:
What men call gallantry, and gods adultery,
Is much more common where the climate's sultry.

64

Happy the nations of the moral north!
  Where all is virtue, and the winter season
Sends sin, without a rag on, shivering forth;
  ('Twas snow that brought St. Anthony to reason);
Where juries cast up what a wife is worth
  By laying whate'er sum, in mulct, they please on
The lover, who must pay a handsome price,
Because it is a marketable vice.

65

Alfonso was the name of Julia's lord,
  A man well looking for his years, and who
Was neither much beloved nor yet abhorr'd;
  They lived together as most people do,
Suffering each other's foibles by accord,
  And not exactly either *one* or *two;*
Yet he was jealous, though he did not show it,
For jealousy dislikes the world to know it.

69

Juan she saw, and, as a pretty child,
  Caress'd him often, such a thing might be
Quite innocently done, and harmless styled,
  When she had twenty years, and thirteen he;
But I am not so sure I should have smiled
  When he was sixteen, Julia twenty-three,
These few short years make wondrous alterations,
Particularly amongst sunburnt nations.

70

Whate'er the cause might be, they had become
    Changed; for the dame grew distant, the youth shy,
Their looks cast down, their greetings almost dumb,
    And much embarrassment in either eye;
There surely will be little doubt with some
    That Donna Julia knew the reason why,
But as for Juan, he had no more notion
Than he who never saw the sea of ocean.

71

Yet Julia's very coldness still was kind,
    And tremulously gentle her small hand
Withdrew itself from his, but left behind
    A little pressure, thrilling, and so bland
And slight, so very slight, that to the mind
    'Twas but a doubt; but ne'er magician's wand
Wrought change with all Armida's fairy art
Like what this light touch left on Juan's heart.

72

And if she met him, though she smiled no more,
    She look'd a sadness sweeter than her smile,
As if her heart had deeper thoughts in store
    She must not own, but cherish'd more the while,
For that compression in its burning core;
    Even innocence itself has many a wile,
And will not dare to trust itself with truth,
And love is taught hypocrisy from youth.

76

She vow'd she never would see Juan more,
    And next day paid a visit to his mother,
And look'd extremely at the opening door,
    Which, by the Virgin's grace, let in another;

Grateful she was, and yet a little sore—
    Again it opens, it can be no other,
'Tis surely Juan now—No! I'm afraid
That night the Virgin was no further pray'd.

77

She now determined that a virtuous woman
    Should rather face and overcome temptation,
That flight was base and dastardly, and no man
    Should ever give her heart the least sensation;
That is to say, a thought beyond the common
    Preference, that we must feel upon occasion,
For people who are pleasanter than others,
But then they only seem so many brothers.

78

And even if by chance—and who can tell?
    The devil's so very sly—she should discover
That all within was not so very well,
    And, if still free, that such or such a lover
Might please perhaps, a virtuous wife can quell
    Such thoughts, and be the better when they're over;
And if the man should ask, 'tis but denial:
I recommend young ladies to make trial.

79

And then there are such things as love divine,
    Bright and immaculate, unmix'd and pure,
Such as the angels think so very fine,
    And matrons, who would be no less secure,
Platonic, perfect, "just such love as mine":
    Thus Julia said—and thought so, to be sure,
And so I'd have her think, were I the man
On whom her reveries celestial ran.

86

So much for Julia. Now we'll turn to Juan,
Poor little fellow! he had no idea
Of his own case, and never hit the true one;
   In feelings quick as Ovid's Miss Medea,
He puzzled over what he found a new one,
   But not as yet imagined it could be a
Thing quite in course, and not at all alarming,
Which, with a little patience, might grow charming.

90

Young Juan wander'd by the glassy brooks
   Thinking unutterable things; he threw
Himself at length within the leafy nooks
   Where the wild branch of the cork forest grew;
There poets find materials for their books,
   And every now and then we read them through,
So that their plan and prosody are eligible,
Unless, like Wordsworth, they prove unintelligible.

91

He, Juan, (and not Wordsworth) so pursued
   His self—communion with his own high soul,
Until his mighty heart, in its great mood,
   Had mitigated part, though not the whole
Of its disease; he did the best he could
   With things not very subject to control,
And turn'd, without perceiving his condition,
Like Coleridge, into a metaphysician.

92

He thought about himself, and the whole earth,
   Of man the wonderful, and of the stars,
And how the deuce they ever could have birth;
   And then he thought of earthquakes, and of wars,

How many miles the moon might have in girth,
  Of air balloons, and of the many bars
To perfect knowledge of the boundless skies;
And then he thought of Donna Julia's eyes.

93

In thoughts like these true wisdom may discern
  Longings sublime, and aspirations high,
Which some are born with, but the most part learn
  To plague themselves withal, they know not why:
'Twas strange that one so young should thus concern
  His brain about the action of the sky;
If *you* think 'twas philosophy that this did,
I can't help thinking puberty assisted.

94

He pored upon the leaves, and on the flowers,
  And heard a voice in all the winds; and then
He thought of wood nymphs and immortal bowers,
  And how the goddesses came down to men:
He miss'd the pathway, he forgot the hours,
  And when he look'd upon his watch again,
He found how much old Time had been a winner—
He also found that he had lost his dinner.

103

'Twas on a summer's day—the sixth of June—
  I like to be particular in dates,
Not only of the age, and year, but moon;
  They are a sort of post house, where the Fates
Change horses, making history change its tune,
  Then spur away o'er empires and o'er states,
Leaving at last not much besides chronology,
Excepting the post-obits of theology.

104

'Twas on the sixth of June, about the hour
    Of half-past six—perhaps still nearer seven,
When Julia sate within as pretty a bower
    As e'er held houri in that heathenish heaven
Described by Mahomet, and Anacreon Moore,
    To whom the lyre and laurels have been given,
With all the trophies of triumphant song—
He won them well, and may he wear them long!

105

She sate, but not alone; I know not well
    How this same interview had taken place,
And even if I knew, I should not tell—
    People should hold their tongues in any case;
No matter how or why the thing befell,
    But there were she and Juan, face to face—
When two such faces are so, 'twould be wise,
But very difficult, to shut their eyes.

106

How beautiful she look'd! her conscious heart
    Glow'd in her cheek, and yet she felt no wrong.
Oh Love! how perfect is thy mystic art,
    Strengthening the weak, and trampling on the strong,
How self-deceitful is the sagest part
    Of mortals whom thy lure hath led along—
The precipice she stood on was immense,
So was her creed in her own innocence.

107

She thought of her own strength, and Juan's youth,
    And of the folly of all prudish fears,
Victorious virtue, and domestic truth,
    And then of Don Alfonso's fifty years;

I wish these last had not occurr'd, in sooth,
　　Because that number rarely much endears,
And through all climes, the snowy and the sunny,
Sounds ill in love, whate'er it may in money.

113

The sun set, and up rose the yellow moon:
　　The devil's in the moon for mischief; they
Who call'd her CHASTE, methinks, began too soon
　　Their nomenclature; there is not a day,
The longest, not the twenty-first of June,
　　Sees half the business in a wicked way
On which three single hours of moonshine smile—
And then she looks so modest all the while.

114

There is a dangerous silence in that hour,
　　A stillness, which leaves room for the full soul
To open all itself, without the power
　　Of calling wholly back its self-control;
The silver light which, hallowing tree and tower,
　　Sheds beauty and deep softness o'er the whole,
Breathes also to the heart, and o'er it throws
A loving languor, which is not repose.

115

And Julia sate with Juan, half embraced
　　And half retiring from the glowing arm,
Which trembled like the bosom where 'twas placed;
　　Yet still she must have thought there was no harm,
Or else 'twere easy to withdraw her waist;
　　But then the situation had its charm,
And then——God knows what next—I can't go on;
I'm almost sorry that I e'er begun.

116

Oh Plato! Plato! you have paved the way,
  With your confounded fantasies, to more
Immoral conduct by the fancied sway
  Your system feigns o'er the controlless core
Of human hearts, than all the long array
  Of poets and romancers—You're a bore,
A charlatan, a coxcomb—and have been,
At best, no better than a go-between.

117

And Julia's voice was lost, except in sighs,
  Until too late for useful conversation;
The tears were gushing from her gentle eyes,
  I wish, indeed, they had not had occasion,
But who, alas! can love, and then be wise?
  Not that remorse did not oppose temptation,
A little still she strove, and much repented,
And whispering "I will ne'er consent"—consented.

126

'Tis sweet to win, no matter how, one's laurels
  By blood or ink; 'tis sweet to put an end
To strife; 'tis sometimes sweet to have our quarrels,
  Particularly with a tiresome friend;
Sweet is old wine in bottles, ale in barrels;
  Dear is the helpless creature we defend
Against the world; and dear the schoolboy spot
We ne'er forget, though there we are forgot.

127

But sweeter still than this, than these, than all,
  Is first and passionate love—it stands alone,
Like Adam's recollection of his fall;
  The tree of knowledge has been pluck'd—all's known—

And life yields nothing further to recall
　　Worthy of this ambrosial sin, so shown,
No doubt in fable, as the unforgiven
　　Fire which Prometheus filch'd for us from heaven.

133

Man's a phenomenon, one knows not what,
　　And wonderful beyond all wondrous measure;
'Tis pity though, in this sublime world, that
　　Pleasure's a sin, and sometimes sin's a pleasure;
Few mortals know what end they would be at,
　　But whether glory, power, or love, or treasure,
The path is through perplexing ways, and when
The goal is gain'd, we die, you know—and then——

134

What then?—I do not know, no more do you—
　　And so good night—Return we to our story:
'Twas in November, when fine days are few,
　　And the far mountains wax a little hoary,
And clap a white cape on their mantles blue;
　　And the sea dashes round the promontory,
And the loud breaker boils against the rock,
And sober suns must set at five o'clock.

135

'Twas, as the watchmen say, a cloudy night;
　　No moon, no stars, the wind was low or loud
By gusts, and many a sparkling hearth was bright
　　With the piled wood, round which the family crowd;
There's something cheerful in that sort of light,
　　Even as a summer sky's without a cloud:
I'm fond of fire, and crickets, and all that,
A lobster salad, and champagne, and chat.

136

'Twas midnight—Donna Julia was in bed,
  Sleeping, most probably—when at her door
Arose a clatter might awake the dead,
If they had never been awoke before,
And that they have been so we all have read,
  And are to be so, at the least, once more—
The door was fasten'd, but with voice and fist
First knocks were heard, then "Madam—Madam—hist!"

137

"For God's sake, Madam—Madam—here's my master,
  With more than half the city at his back—
Was ever heard of such a cursed disaster!
  'Tis not my fault—I kept good watch—Alack!
Do, pray undo the bolt a little faster—
  They're on the stair just now, and in a crack
Will all be here; perhaps he yet may fly—
Surely the window's not so *very* high!"

138

By this time Don Alfonso was arrived,
  With torches, friends, and servants in great number;
The major part of them had long been wived,
  And therefore paused not to disturb the slumber
Of any wicked woman, who contrived
  By stealth her husband's temples to encumber:
Examples of this kind are so contagious,
Were *one* not punish'd, *all* would be outrageous.

139

I can't tell how, or why, or what suspicion
  Could enter into Don Alfonso's head;
But for a cavalier of his condition
  It surely was exceedingly ill-bred,

Without a word of previous admonition,
   To hold a levee round his lady's bed,
And summon lackeys, arm'd with fire and sword,
   To prove himself the thing he most abhorr'd.

140

Poor Donna Julia! starting as from sleep,
   (Mind—that I do not say—she had not slept)
Began at once to scream, and yawn, and weep;
   Her maid Antonia, who was an adept,
Contrived to fling the bedclothes in a heap,
   As if she had just now from out them crept:
I can't tell why she should take all this trouble
To prove her mistress had been sleeping double.

141

But Julia mistress, and Antonia maid,
   Appear'd like two poor harmless women, who
Of goblins, but still more of men afraid,
   Had thought one man might be deterr'd by two,
And therefore side by side were gently laid,
   Until the hours of absence should run through,
And truant husband should return, and say,
"My dear, I was the first who came away."

142

Now Julia found at length a voice, and cried,
   "In heaven's name, Don Alfonso, what d'ye mean?
Has madness seized you? would that I had died
   Ere such a monster's victim I had been!
What may this midnight violence betide,
   A sudden fit of drunkenness or spleen?
Dare you suspect me, whom the thought would kill?
Search, then, the room!"—Alfonso said, "I will."

He search'd, *they* search'd, and rummaged everywhere,
 Closet and clothes'-press, chest and windowseat,
And found much linen, lace, and several pair
 Of stockings, slippers, brushes, combs, complete,
With other articles of ladies fair,
 To keep them beautiful, or leave them neat:
Arras they prick'd and curtains with their swords,
And wounded several shutters, and some boards.

Under the bed they search'd, and there they found—
 No matter what—it was not that they sought;
They open'd windows, gazing if the ground
 Had signs or footmarks, but the earth said naught;
And then they stared each other's faces round:
 'Tis odd, not one of all these seekers thought,
And seems to me almost a sort of blunder,
Of looking *in* the bed as well as under.

During this inquisition Julia's tongue
 Was not asleep—"Yes, search and search," she cried,
"Insult on insult heap, and wrong on wrong!
 It was for this that I became a bride!
For this in silence I have suffer'd long
 A husband like Alfonso at my side;
But now I'll bear no more, nor here remain,
If there be law, or lawyers, in all Spain.

"Yes, Don Alfonso! husband now no more,
 If ever you indeed deserved the name,
Is't worthy of your years?—you have threescore,
 Fifty, or sixty—it is all the same—

Is't wise or fitting causeless to explore
  For facts against a virtuous woman's fame?
Ungrateful, perjured, barbarous Don Alfonso,
  How dare you think your lady would go on so?"

159

The Senhor Don Alfonso stood confused;
  Antonia bustled round the ransack'd room,
And, turning up her nose, with looks abused
  Her master, and his myrmidons, of whom
Not one, except the attorney, was amused;
  He, like Achates, faithful to the tomb,
So there were quarrels, cared not for the cause,
Knowing they must be settled by the laws.

160

With prying snub-nose, and small eyes, he stood,
  Following Antonia's motions here and there,
With much suspicion in his attitude;
  For reputations he had little care;
So that a suit or action were made good,
  Small pity had he for the young and fair,
And ne'er believed in negatives, till these
Were proved by competent false witnesses.

161

But Don Alfonso stood with downcast looks,
  And, truth to say, he made a foolish figure;
When, after searching in five hundred nooks,
  And treating a young wife with so much rigor,
He gain'd no point, except some self-rebukes,
  Added to those his lady with such vigor
Had pour'd upon him for the last half-hour,
Quick, thick, and heavy—as a thundershower.

162

At first he tried to hammer an excuse,
  To which the sole reply were tears, and sobs,
And indications of hysterics, whose
  Prologue is always certain throes, and throbs,
Gasps, and whatever else the owners choose—
  Alfonso saw his wife, and thought of Job's;
He saw too, in perspective, her relations,
And then he tried to muster all his patience.

163

He stood in act to speak, or rather stammer,
  But sage Antonia cut him short before
The anvil of his speech received the hammer,
  With "Pray sir, leave the room, and say no more,
Or madam dies."—Alfonso mutter'd "D—n her,"
  But nothing else, the time of words was o'er;
He cast a rueful look or two, and did,
He knew not wherefore, that which he was bid.

164

With him retired his *"posse comitatus,"*
  The attorney last, who linger'd near the door,
Reluctantly, still tarrying there as late as
  Antonia let him—not a little sore
At this most strange and unexplain'd *"hiatus"*
  In Don Alfonso's facts, which just now wore
An awkward look; as he revolved the case
The door was fasten'd in his legal face.

165

No sooner was it bolted, than—Oh shame!
  Oh sin! Oh sorrow! and Oh womankind!
How can you do such things and keep your fame,
  Unless this world, and t'other too, be blind?

Nothing so dear as an unfilch'd good name!
But to proceed—for there is more behind:
With much heartfelt reluctance be it said,
Young Juan slipp'd, half-smother'd, from the bed.

166

He had been hid—I don't pretend to say
    How, nor can I indeed describe the where—
Young, slender, and pack'd easily, he lay,
    No doubt, in little compass, round or square;
But pity him I neither must nor may
    His suffocation by that pretty pair;
'Twere better, sure, to die so, than be shut
With maudlin Clarence in his Malmsey butt.

169

What's to be done? Alfonso will be back
    The moment he has sent his fools away.
Antonia's skill was put upon the rack,
    But no device could be brought into play—
And how to parry the renew'd attack?
    Besides, it wanted but few hours of day:
Antonia puzzled; Julia did not speak,
But press'd her bloodless lip to Juan's cheek.

170

He turn'd his lip to hers, and with his hand
    Call'd back the tangles of her wandering hair;
Even then their love they could not all command,
    And half forgot their danger and despair:
Antonia's patience now was at a stand—
    "Come, come, 'tis no time now for fooling there,"
She whisper'd, in great wrath—"I must deposit
This pretty gentleman within the closet:"

173

Now, Don Alfonso entering, but alone,
　　Closed the oration of the trusty maid:
She loiter'd, and he told her to be gone,
　　An order somewhat sullenly obey'd;
However, present remedy was none,
　　And no great good seem'd answer'd if she stayed:
Regarding both with slow and sidelong view,
She snuff'd the candle, curtsied, and withdrew.

174

Alfonso paused a minute—then begun
　　Some strange excuses for his late proceeding;
He would not justify what he had done,
　　To say the best, it was extreme ill-breeding;
But there were ample reasons for it, none
　　Of which he specified in this his pleading:
His speech was a fine sample, on the whole,
Of rhetoric, which the learn'd call *"rigmarole."*

180

Alfonso closed his speech, and begg'd her pardon,
　　Which Julia half withheld, and then half granted,
And laid conditions, he thought, very hard on,
　　Denying several little things he wanted:
He stood like Adam lingering near his garden,
　　With useless penitence perplex'd and haunted,
Beseeching she no further would refuse,
When lo! he stumbled o'er a pair of shoes.

181

A pair of shoes!—what then? not much, if they
　　Are such a fit with lady's feet, but these
(No one can tell how much I grieve to say)
　　Were masculine; to see them, and to seize,

Was but a moment's act—Ah! Well-a-day!
My teeth begin to chatter, my veins freeze—
Alfonso first examined well their fashion,
And then flew out into another passion.

182

He left the room for his relinquish'd sword,
    And Julia instant to the closet flew.
"Fly, Juan, fly! for heaven's sake—not a word—
    The door is open—you may yet slip through
The passage you so often have explored—
    Here is the garden key—Fly—fly—Adieu!
Haste—haste!—I hear Alfonso's hurrying feet—
Day has not broke—there's no one in the street."

183

None can say that this was not good advice,
    The only mischief was, it came too late;
Of all experience 'tis the usual price,
    A sort of income tax laid on by fate:
Juan had reach'd the room door in a trice,
    And might have done so by the garden gate,
But met Alfonso in his dressing gown,
Who threaten'd death—so Juan knock'd him down.

184

Dire was the scuffle, and out went the light,
    Antonia cried out "Rape!" and Julia "Fire!"
But not a servant stirr'd to aid the fight.
    Alfonso, pommell'd to his heart's desire,
Swore lustily he'd be revenged this night;
    And Juan, too, blasphemed an octave higher,
His blood was up; though young, he was a Tartar,
And not at all disposed to prove a martyr.

185

Alfonso's sword had dropp'd ere he could draw it,
    And they continued battling hand to hand,
For Juan very luckily ne'er saw it;
    His temper not being under great command,
If at that moment he had chanced to claw it,
    Alfonso's days had not been in the land
Much longer—Think of husbands', lovers' lives!
And how ye may be doubly widows—wives!

186

Alfonso grappled to detain the foe,
    And Juan throttled him to get away,
And blood ('twas from the nose) began to flow;
    At last, as they more faintly wrestling lay,
Juan contrived to give an awkward blow,
    And then his only garment quite gave way;
He fled, like Joseph, leaving it; but there,
I doubt, all likeness ends between the pair.

187

Lights came at length, and men, and maids, who found
    An awkward spectacle their eyes before;
Antonia in hysterics, Julia swoon'd,
    Alfonso leaning, breathless, by the door;
Some half-torn drapery scatter'd on the ground,
    Some blood, and several footsteps, but no more:
Juan the gate gain'd, turn'd the key about,
And liking not the inside, lock'd the out.

188

Here ends this canto—Need I sing, or say,
    How Juan, naked, favor'd by the night,
Who favors what she should not, found his way,
    And reach'd his home in an unseemly plight?

The pleasant scandal which arose next day,
   The nine days' wonder which was brought to light,
And how Alfonso sued for a divorce,
   Were in the English newspapers, of course.

189

If you would like to see the whole proceedings,
   The depositions, and the cause at full,
The names of all the witnesses, the pleadings
   Of counsel to nonsuit, or to annul,
There's more than one edition, and the readings
   Are various, but they none of them are dull,
The best is that in shorthand ta'en by Gurney,
Who to Madrid on purpose made a journey.

190

But Donna Inez, to divert the train
   Of one of the most circulating scandals
That had for centuries been known in Spain,
   Since Roderic's Goths, or older Genseric's Vandals,
First vow'd (and never had she vow'd in vain)
   To Virgin Mary several pounds of candles;
And then, by the advice of some old ladies,
She sent her son to be embark'd at Cadiz.

191

She had resolved that he should travel through
   All European climes, by land or sea,
To mend his former morals, or get new,
   Especially in France and Italy,
(At least this is the thing most people do).
   Julia was sent into a nunnery,
And there, perhaps, her feelings may be better
Shown in the following copy of her letter:

192

"They tell me 'tis decided; you depart:
  'Tis wise—'tis well, but not the less a pain;
I have no further claim on your young heart,
  Mine was the victim, and would be again;
To love too much has been the only art
  I used—I write in haste, and if a stain
Be on this sheet, 'tis not what it appears,
My eyeballs burn and throb, but have no tears.

193

"I loved, I love you, for that love have lost
  State, station, heaven, mankind's, my own esteem,
And yet can not regret what it hath cost,
  So dear is still the memory of that dream;
Yet, if I name my guilt, 'tis not to boast,
  None can deem harshlier of me than I deem:
I trace this scrawl because I cannot rest—
I've nothing to reproach, nor to request.

194

"Man's love is of his life a thing apart,
  'Tis woman's whole existence; man may range
The court, camp, church, the vessel, and the mart,
  Sword, gown, gain, glory, offer in exchange
Pride, fame, ambition, to fill up his heart,
  And few there are whom these can not estrange;
Man has all these resources, we but one,
To love again, and be again undone."

198

This note was written upon gilt-edged paper
  With a neat crow quill, rather hard, but new;
Her small white fingers scarce could reach the taper,
  But trembled as magnetic needles do,

And yet she did not let one tear escape her;
  The seal a sunflower; *"Elle vous suit partout"*
The motto, cut upon a white cornelian;
  The wax was superfine, its hue vermilion.

199

This was Don Juan's earliest scrape; but whether
  I shall proceed with his adventures is
Dependent on the public altogether;
  We'll see, however, what they say to this,
Their favor in an author's cap's a feather,
  And no great mischief's done by their caprice;
And if their approbation we experience,
Perhaps they'll have some more about a year hence.

200

My poem's epic, and is meant to be
  Divided in twelve books; each book containing,
With love, and war, a heavy gale at sea,
  A list of ships, and captains, and kings reigning,
New characters; the episodes are three:
  A panorama view of hews in training,
After the style of Virgil and of Homer,
So that my name of Epic's no misnomer.

201

All these things will be specified in time,
  With strict regard to Aristotle's rules,
The *vade mecum* of the true sublime,
  Which makes so many poets, and some fools;
Prose poets like blank verse, I'm fond of rhyme,
  Good workmen never quarrel with their tools;
I've got new mythological machinery,
And very handsome supernatural scenery.

202

There's only one slight difference between
    Me and my epic brethren gone before,
And here the advantage is my own, I ween;
    (Not that I have not several merits more,
But this will more peculiarly be seen)
    They so embellish, that 'tis quite a bore
Their labyrinth of fables to thread through,
Whereas this story's actually true.

203

If any person doubt it, I appeal
    To history, tradition, and to facts,
To newspapers, whose truth all know and feel,
    To plays in five, and operas in three acts;
All these confirm my statement a good deal,
    But that which more completely faith exacts
Is, that myself, and several now in Seville,
Saw Juan's last elopement with the devil.

204

If ever I should condescend to prose,
    I'll write poetical commandments, which
Shall supersede beyond all doubt all those
    That went before; in these I shall enrich
My text with many things that no one knows,
    And carry precept to the highest pitch:
I'll call the work "Longinus o'er a Bottle,
Or, Every Poet his *own* Aristotle."

205

Thou shalt believe in Milton, Dryden, Pope;
    Thou shalt not set up Wordsworth, Coleridge, Southey;
Because the first is crazed beyond all hope,
    The second drunk, the third so quaint and mouthey:

With Crabbe it may be difficult to cope,
  And Campbell's Hippocrene is somewhat drouthy:
Thou shalt not steal from Samuel Rogers, nor
  Commit—flirtation with the muse of Moore.

206

Thou shalt not covet Mr. Sotheby's Muse,
  His Pegasus, nor anything that's his;
Thou shalt not bear false witness like "the Blues,"
  (There's one, at least, is very fond of this);
Thou shalt not write, in short, but what I choose:
  This is true criticism, and you may kiss—
Exactly as you please, or not, the rod,
But if you don't, I'll lay it on, by G—d!

207

If any person should presume to assert
  This story is not moral, first, I pray,
That they will not cry out before they're hurt,
  Then that they'll read it o'er again, and say,
(But, doubtless, nobody will be so pert)
  That this is not a moral tale, though gay;
Besides, in canto twelfth, I mean to show
The very place where wicked people go.

213

But now at thirty years my hair is gray—
  (I wonder what it will be like at forty?
I thought of a peruke the other day)
  My heart is not much greener; and, in short, I
Have squander'd my whole summer while 'twas May,
  And feel no more the spirit to retort; I
Have spent my life, both interest and principal,
And deem not, what I deem'd, my soul invincible.

214

No more—no more—Oh! nevermore on me
   The freshness of the heart can fall like dew,
Which out of all the lovely things we see
Extracts emotions beautiful and new,
Hived in our bosoms like the bag o' the bee:
   Think'st thou the honey with those objects grew?
Alas! 'twas not in them, but in thy power
To double even the sweetness of a flower.

215

No more—no more—Oh! nevermore, my heart,
   Canst thou be my sole world, my universe!
Once all in all, but now a thing apart,
   Thou canst not be my blessing or my curse:
The illusion's gone forever, and thou art
   Insensible, I trust, but none the worse,
And in thy stead I've got a deal of judgment,
Though heaven knows how it ever found a lodgement.

216

My days of love are over, me no more
   The charms of maid, wife, and still less of widow,
Can make the fool of which they made before,
   In short, I must not lead the life I did do;
The credulous hope of mutual minds is o'er,
   The copious use of claret is forbid too,
So for a good old-gentlemanly vice,
I think I must take up with avarice.

219

What are the hopes of man? old Egypt's King
   Cheops erected the first pyramid
And largest, thinking it was just the thing
   To keep his memory whole, and mummy hid;

But somebody or other rummaging,
  Burglariously broke his coffin's lid:
Let not a monument give you or me hopes,
Since not a pinch of dust remains of Cheops.

220

But I being fond of true philosophy,
  Say very often to myself, "Alas!
All things that have been born were born to die,
  And flesh (which Death mows down to hay) is grass;
You've pass'd your youth not so unpleasantly,
  And if you had it o'er again—'twould pass—
So thank your stars that matters are no worse,
And read your Bible, sir, and mind your purse."

221

But for the present, gentle reader! and
  Still gentler purchaser! the bard—that's I—
Must, with permission, shake you by the hand,
  And so your humble servant, and goodbye!
We meet again, if we should understand
  Each other; and if not, I shall not try
Your patience further than by this short sample—
'Twere well if others follow'd my example.

222

"Go, little book, from this my solitude!
  I cast thee on the waters, go thy ways!
And if, as I believe, thy vein be good,
  The world will find thee after many days."
When Southey's read, and Wordsworth understood,
  I can't help putting in my claim to praise—
The four first rhymes are Southey's every line:
For God's sake, reader! take them not for mine.

From CANTO II

8

But to our tale: the Donna Inez sent
    Her son to Cadiz only to embark;
To stay there had not answer'd her intent,
    But why?—we leave the reader in the dark—
'Twas for a voyage that the young man was meant,
    As if a Spanish ship were Noah's ark,
To wean him from the wickedness of earth,
And send him like a dove of promise forth.

9

Don Juan bade his valet pack his things
    According to direction, then received
A lecture and some money: for four springs
    He was to travel; and though Inez grieved,
(As every kind of parting has its stings)
    She hoped he would improve—perhaps believed:
A letter, too, she gave (he never read it)
Of good advice—and two or three of credit.

11

Juan embark'd—the ship got under way,
    The wind was fair, the water passing rough;
A devil of a sea rolls in that bay,
    As I, who've cross'd it oft, know well enough;
And, standing upon deck, the dashing spray
    Flies in one's face, and makes it weather-tough:
And there he stood to take, and take again,
His first—perhaps his last—farewell of Spain.

12

I can't but say it is an awkward sight
   To see one's native land receding through
The growing waters; it unmans one quite,
   Especially when life is rather new:
I recollect Great Britain's coast looks white,
   But almost every other country's blue,
When gazing on them, mystified by distance,
We enter on our nautical existence.

17

And Juan wept, and much he sigh'd and thought,
   While his salt tears dropp'd into the salt sea,
"Sweets to the sweet"; (I like so much to quote;
   You must excuse this extract, 'tis where she,
The Queen of Denmark, for Ophelia brought
   Flowers to the grave); and, sobbing often, he
Reflected on his present situation,
And seriously resolved on reformation.

18

"Farewell, my Spain! a long farewell!" he cried,
   "Perhaps I may revisit thee no more,
But die, as many an exiled heart hath died,
   Of its own thirst to see again thy shore:
Farewell, where Guadalquivir's waters glide!
   Farewell, my mother! and, since all is o'er,
Farewell, too dearest Julia!"—(here he drew
Her letter out again, and read it through).

19

"And oh! if e'er I should forget, I swear—
   But that's impossible, and cannot be—
Sooner shall this blue ocean melt to air,
   Sooner shall earth resolve itself to sea,

Than I resign thine image, Oh! my fair!
    Or think of anything excepting thee;
A mind diseased no remedy can physic—"
    (Here the ship gave a lurch, and he grew seasick.)

20

"Sooner shall heaven kiss earth"—(here he fell sicker)
    "Oh, Julia! what is every other woe?—
(For God's sake let me have a glass of liquor,
    Pedro, Battista, help me down below).
Julia, my love!—(you rascal, Pedro, quicker)—
    Oh Julia!—(this cursed vessel pitches so)—
Beloved Julia, hear me still beseeching!"
(Here he grew inarticulate with reaching.)

21

He felt that chilling heaviness of heart,
    Or rather stomach, which, alas! attends,
Beyond the best apothecary's art,
    The loss of love, the treachery of friends,
Or death of those we dote on, when apart
    Of us dies with them as each fond hope ends:
No doubt he would have been much more pathetic,
But the sea acted as a strong emetic.

103

As they drew nigh the land, which now was seen
    Unequal in its aspect here and there,
They felt the freshness of its growing green,
    That waved in forest tops, and smooth'd the air,
And fell upon their glazed eyes like a screen
    From glistening waves, and skies so hot and bare—
Lovely seem'd any object that should sweep
Away the vast, salt, dread, eternal deep.

104

The shore look'd wild, without a trace of man,
 And girt by formidable waves; but they
Were made for land, and thus their course they ran,
 Though right ahead the roaring breakers lay:
A reef between them also now began
 To show its boiling surf and bounding spray,
But finding no place for their landing better,
They ran the boat for shore, and overset her.

105

But in his native stream, the Guadalquivir,
 Juan to lave his youthful limbs was wont;
And having learnt to swim in that sweet river,
 Had often turn'd the art to some account:
A better swimmer you could scarce see ever,
 He could, perhaps, have pass'd the Hellespont,
As once (a feat on which ourselves we prided)
Leander, Mr. Ekenhead, and I did.

106

So here, though faint, emaciated, and stark,
 He buoy'd his boyish limbs, and strove to ply
With the quick wave, and gain, ere it was dark,
 The beach which lay before him, high and dry:
The greatest danger here was from a shark,
 That carried off his neighbor by the thigh;
As for the other two they could not swim,
So nobody arrived on shore but him.

107

Nor yet had he arrived but for the oar,
 Which, providentially for him, was wash'd
Just as his feeble arms could strike no more,
 And the hard wave o'erwhelm'd him as 'twas dash'd

Within his grasp; he clung to it, and sore
   The waters beat while he thereto was lash'd;
At last, with swimming, wading, scrambling, he
   Roll'd on the beach, half senseless, from the sea:

108

There, breathless, with his digging nails he clung
   Fast to the sand, lest the returning wave,
From whose reluctant roar his life he wrung,
   Should suck him back to her insatiate grave:
And there he lay, full length, where he was flung,
   Before the entrance of a cliff-worn cave,
With just enough of life to feel its pain,
And deem that it was saved, perhaps, in vain.

109

With slow and staggering effort he arose,
   But sunk again upon his bleeding knee
And quivering hand; and then he look'd for those
   Who long had been his mates upon the sea,
But none of them appear'd to share his woes,
   Save one, a corpse from out the famish'd three,
Who died two days before, and now had found
An unknown barren beach for burial ground.

110

And as he gazed, his dizzy brain spun fast,
   And down he sunk; and as he sunk, the sand
Swam round and round, and all his senses pass'd:
   He fell upon his side, and his stretch'd hand
Droop'd dripping on the oar, (their jury mast)
   And, like a wither'd lily, on the land
His slender frame and pallid aspect lay,
As fair a thing as e'er was form'd of clay.

111

How long in his damp trance young Juan lay
    He knew not, for the earth was gone for him,
And Time had nothing more of night nor day
    For his congealing blood, and senses dim;
And how this heavy faintness pass'd away
    He knew not, till each painful pulse and limb,
And tingling vein, seem'd throbbing back to life,
For Death, though vanquish'd, still retired with strife.

112

His eyes he open'd, shut, again unclosed,
    For all was doubt and dizziness; methought
He still was in the boat, and had but dozed,
    And felt again with his despair o'erwrought,
And wish'd it death in which he had reposed,
    And then once more his feelings back were brought,
And slowly by his swimming eyes was seen
A lovely female face of seventeen.

113

'Twas bending close o'er his, and the small mouth
    Seem'd almost prying into his for breath;
And chafing him, the soft warm hand of youth
    Recall'd his answering spirits back from death;
And, bathing his chill temples, tried to soothe
    Each pulse to animation, till beneath
Its gentle touch and trembling care, a sigh
To these kind efforts made a low reply.

114

Then was the cordial pour'd, and mantle flung
    Around his scarce-clad limbs; and the fair arm
Raised higher the faint head which o'er it hung;
    And her transparent cheek, all pure and warm,

Pillow'd his deathlike forehead; then she wrung
   His dewy curls, long drench'd by every storm;
And watch'd with eagerness each throb that drew
A sigh from his heaved bosom—and hers, too.

115

And lifting him with care into the cave,
   The gentle girl, and her attendant—one
Young, yet her elder, and of brow less grave,
   And more robust of figure—then begun
To kindle fire, and as the new flames gave
   Light to the rocks that roof'd them, which the sun
Had never seen, the maid, or whatsoe'er
She was, appear'd distinct, and tall, and fair.

116

Her brow was overhung with coins of gold,
   That sparkled o'er the auburn of her hair,
Her clustering hair, whose longer locks were roll'd
   In braids behind, and though her stature were
Even of the highest for a female mold,
   They nearly reach'd her heel; and in her air
There was a something which bespoke command,
As one who was a lady in the land.

117

Her hair, I said, was auburn; but her eyes
   Were black as death, their lashes the same hue,
Of downcast length, in whose silk shadow lies
   Deepest attraction, for when to the view
Forth from its raven fringe the full glance flies,
   Ne'er with such force the swiftest arrow flew;
'Tis as the snake late coil'd, who pours his length,
And hurls at once his venom and his strength.

123

And these two tended him, and cheer'd him both
   With food and raiment, and those soft attentions,
Which are (as I must own) of female growth,
   And have ten thousand delicate inventions:
They made a most superior mess of broth,
   A thing which poesy but seldom mentions,
But the best dish that e'er was cook'd since Homer's
Achilles order'd dinner for newcomers.

124

I'll tell you who they were, this female pair,
   Lest they should seem princesses in disguise;
Besides, I hate all mystery, and that air
   Of claptrap, which your recent poets prize;
And so, in short, the girls they really were
   They shall appear before your curious eyes,
Mistress and maid; the first was only daughter
Of an old man, who lived upon the water.

125

A fisherman he had been in his youth,
   And still a sort of fisherman was he;
But other speculations were, in sooth,
   Added to his connection with the sea,
Perhaps not so respectable, in truth:
   A little smuggling, and some piracy,
Left him, at last, the sole of many masters
Of an ill-gotten million of piasters.

126

A fisher, therefore, was he—though of men,
   Like Peter the Apostle—and he fish'd
For wandering merchant vessels, now and then,
   And sometimes caught as many as he wish'd;

The cargoes he confiscated, and gain
    He sought in the slave market too, and dish'd
Full many a morsel for that Turkish trade,
    By which, no doubt, a good deal may be made.

127

He was a Greek, and on his isle had built
    (One of the wild and smaller Cyclades)
A very handsome house from out his guilt,
    And there he lived exceedingly at ease;
Heaven knows what cash he got, or blood he spilt,
    A sad old fellow was he, if you please,
But this I know, it was a spacious building,
Full of barbaric carving, paint, and gilding.

128

He had an only daughter, call'd Haidee,
    The greatest heiress of the Eastern Isles;
Besides, so very beautiful was she,
    Her dowry was as nothing to her smiles:
Still in her teens, and like a lovely tree
    She grew to womanhood, and between whiles
Rejected several suitors, just to learn
How to accept a better in his turn.

129

And walking out upon the beach, below
    The cliff, towards sunset, on that day she found,
Insensible—not dead, but nearly so—
    Don Juan, almost famish'd, and half drown'd;
But being naked, she was shock'd, you know,
    Yet deem'd herself in common pity bound,
As far as in her lay, "to take him in,
A stranger" dying, with so white a skin.

130

But taking him into her father's house
   Was not exactly the best way to save,
But like conveying to the cat the mouse,
   Or people in a trance into their grave;
Because the good old man had so much "vous,"
   Unlike the honest Arab thieves so brave,
He would have hospitably cured the stranger,
And sold him instantly when out of danger.

And therefore, with her maid, she thought it best
   (A virgin always on her maid relies)
To place him in the cave for present rest:
   And when, at last, he open'd his black eyes,
Their charity increased about their guest;
   And their compassion grew to such a size,
It open'd half the turnpike gates to heaven—
(St. Paul says 'tis the toll which must be given).

And Haidee met the morning face to face;
   Her own was freshest, though a feverish flush
Had dyed it with the headlong blood, whose race
   From heart to cheek is curb'd into a blush,
Like to a torrent which a mountain's base,
   That overpowers some alpine river's rush,
Checks to a lake, whose waves in circles spread;
Or the Red Sea—but the sea is not red.

And down the cliff the island virgin came,
   And near the cave her quick light footsteps drew,
While the sun smiled on her with his first flame,
   And young Aurora kiss'd her lips with dew,

Taking her for sister; just the same
   Mistake you would have made on seeing the two,
Although the mortal, quite as fresh and fair,
Had all the advantage too of not being air.

143

And when into the cavern Haidee stepp'd
   All timidly, yet rapidly, she saw
That like an infant Juan sweetly slept;
   And then she stopp'd, and stood as if in awe,
(For sleep is awful) and on tiptoe crept
   And wrapped him closer, lest the air, too raw,
Should reach his blood, then o'er him still as death
Bent, with hush'd lips, that drank his scarce-drawn breath.

148

And she bent o'er him, and he lay beneath,
   Hush'd as the babe upon its mother's breast,
Droop'd as the willow when no winds can breathe,
   Lull'd like the depth of ocean when at rest,
Fair as the crowning rose of the whole wreath,
   Soft as the callow cygnet in its nest;
In short, he was a very pretty fellow,
Although his woes had turn'd him rather yellow.

149

He woke and gazed, and would have slept again,
   But the fair face which met his eyes forbade
Those eyes to close, though weariness and pain
   Had further sleep a further pleasure made;
For woman's face was never form'd in vain
   For Juan, so that even when he pray'd
He turn'd from grisly saints, and martyrs hairy,
To the sweet portraits of the Virgin Mary.

150

And thus upon his elbow he arose,
    And look'd upon the lady, in whose cheek
The pale contended with the purple rose,
    As with an effort she began to speak;
Her eyes were eloquent, her words would pose,
    Although she told him, in good modern Greek,
With an Ionian accent, low and sweet,
That he was faint, and must not talk, but eat.

168

And every day by daybreak—rather early
    For Juan, who was somewhat fond of rest—
She came into the cave, but it was merely
    To see her bird reposing in his nest;
And she would softly stir his locks so curly,
    Without disturbing her yet slumbering guest,
Breathing all gently o'er his cheek and mouth,
As o'er a bed of roses the sweet south.

169

And every morn his color freshlier came,
    And every day help'd on his convalescence;
'Twas well, because health in the human frame
    Is pleasant, besides being true love's essence,
For health and idleness to passion's flame
    Are oil and gunpowder; and some good lessons
Are also learnt from Ceres and from Bacchus,
Without whom Venus will not long attack us.

170

While Venus fills the heart (without heart really
    Love, though good always, is not quite so good)
Ceres presents a plate of vermicelli—
    For love must be sustain'd like flesh and blood—

While Bacchus pours out wine, or hands a jelly:
    Eggs, oysters too, are amatory food;
But who is their purveyor from above
Heaven knows—it may be Neptune, Pan, or Jove.

171

When Juan woke he found some good things ready,
    A bath, a breakfast, and the finest eyes
That ever made a youthful heart less steady,
    Besides her maid's, as pretty for their size;
But I have spoken of all this already—
    And repetition's tiresome and unwise—
Well—Juan, after bathing in the sea,
Came always back to coffee and Haidee.

172

Both were so young, and one so innocent,
    That bathing pass'd for nothing; Juan seem'd
To her, as 'twere, the kind of being sent,
    Of whom these two years she had nightly dream'd,
A something to be loved, a creature meant
    To be her happiness, and whom she deem'd
To render happy; all who joy would win
Must share it—Happiness was born a twin.

173

It was such pleasure to behold him, such
    Enlargement of existence to partake
Nature with him, to thrill beneath his touch,
    To watch him slumbering, and to see him wake:
To live with him forever were too much;
    But then the thought of parting made her quake:
He was her own, her ocean treasure, cast
Like a rich wreck—her first love, and her last.

174

And thus a moon roll'd on, and fair Haidee
    Paid daily visits to her boy, and took
Such plentiful precautions, that still he
    Remain'd unknown within his craggy nook;
At last her father's prows put out to sea,
    For certain merchantmen upon the look,
Not as of yore to carry off an Io,
But three Ragusan vessels, bound for Scio.

175

Then came her freedom, for she had no mother,
    So that, her father being at sea, she was
Free as a married woman, or such other
    Female, as where she likes may freely pass,
Without even the incumbrance of a brother,
    The freest she that ever gazed on glass:
I speak of Christian lands in this comparison,
Where wives, at least, are seldom kept in garrison.

176

Now she prolong'd her visits and her talk
    (For they must talk), and he had learnt to say
So much as to propose to take a walk—
    For little had he wander'd since the day
On which, like a young flower snapp'd from the stalk,
    Drooping and dewy on the beach he lay—
And thus they walk'd out in the afternoon,
And saw the sun set opposite the moon.

177

It was a wild and breaker-beaten coast,
    With cliffs above, and a broad sandy shore,
Guarded by shoals and rocks as by an host,
    With here and there a creek, whose aspect wore

A better welcome to the tempest-tossed;
  And rarely ceased the haughty billow's roar,
Save on the dead long summer days, which make
The outstretch'd ocean glitter like a lake.

178

And the small ripple spilt upon the beach
  Scarcely o'erpass'd the cream of your champagne,
When o'er the brim the sparkling bumpers reach,
  That spring dew of the spirit! the heart's rain!
Few things surpass old wine; and they may preach
  Who please—the more because they preach in vain—
Let us have wine and woman, mirth and laughter,
Sermons and soda water the day after.

179

Man, being reasonable, must get drunk;
  The best of life is but intoxication:
Glory, the grape, love, gold, in these are sunk
  The hopes of all men, and of every nation;
Without their sap, how branchless were the trunk
  Of life's strange tree, so fruitful on occasion:
But to return—Get very drunk; and when
You wake with headache, you shall see what then.

180

Ring for your valet—bid him quickly bring
  Some hock and soda water, then you'll know
A pleasure worthy Xerxes the great king;
  For not the blessed sherbet, sublimed with snow,
Nor the first sparkle of the desert spring,
  Nor Burgundy in all its sunset glow,
After long travel, ennui, love, or slaughter,
Vie with that draught of hock and soda water.

181

The coast—I think it was the coast that I
　　Was just describing—Yes, it *was* the coast—
Lay at this period quiet as the sky,
　　The sands untumbled, the blue waves untossed,
And all was stillness, save the seabird's cry,
　　And dolphin's leap, and little billow crossed
By some low rock or shelve, that made it fret
Against the boundary it scarcely wet.

182

And forth they wandered, her sire being gone,
　　As I have said, upon an expedition;
And mother, brother, guardian, she had none,
　　Save Zoe, who, although with due precision
She waited on her lady with the sun,
　　Thought daily service was her only mission,
Bringing warm water, wreathing her long tresses,
And asking now and then for castoff dresses.

183

It was the cooling hour, just when the rounded
　　Red sun sinks down behind the azure hill,
Which then seems as if the whole earth is bounded,
　　Circling all nature, hush'd, and dim, and still,
With the far mountain crescent half surrounded
　　On one side, and the deep sea calm and chill
Upon the other, and the rosy sky,
With one star sparkling through it like an eye.

184

And thus they wander'd forth, and hand in hand,
　　Over the shining pebbles and the shells,
Glided along the smooth and harden'd sand,
　　And in the worn and wild receptacles

Work'd by the storms, yet work'd as it were plann'd,
   In hollow halls, with sparry roofs and cells,
They turn'd to rest; and, each clasp'd by an arm,
   Yielded to the deep twilight's purple charm.

185

They look'd up to the sky, whose floating glow
   Spread like a rosy ocean, vast and bright;
They gazed upon the glittering sea below,
   Whence the broad moon rose circling into sight;
They heard the wave's splash, and the wind so low,
   And saw each other's dark eyes darting light
Into each other—and, beholding this,
Their lips drew near, and clung into a kiss;

186

A long, long kiss, a kiss of youth, and love,
   And beauty, all concentrating like rays
Into one focus, kindled from above;
   Such kisses as belong to early days,
Where heart, and soul, and sense, in concert move,
   And the blood's lava, and the pulse a blaze,
Each kiss a heart-quake—for a kiss's strength,
I think, it must be reckon'd by its length.

187

By length I mean duration; theirs endured
   Heaven knows how long—no doubt they never reckon'd;
And if they had, they could not have secured
   The sum of their sensations to a second:
They had not spoken; but they felt allured,
   As if their souls and lips each other beckon'd,
Which, being join'd, like swarming bees they clung—
Their hearts the flowers from whence the honey sprung.

188

They were alone, but not alone as they
   Who shut in chambers think it loneliness;
The silent ocean, and the starlight bay,
   The twilight glow, which momently grew less,
The voiceless sands, and dropping caves, that lay
   Around them, made them to each other press,
As if there were no life beneath the sky
Save theirs, and that their life could never die.

189

They fear'd no eyes nor ears on that lone beach,
   They felt no terrors from the night, they were
All in all to each other: though their speech
   Was broken words, they *thought* a language there—
And all the burning tongues the passions teach
   Found in one sigh the best interpreter
Of nature's oracle—first love—that all
Which Eve has left her daughters since her fall.

190

Haidee spoke not of scruples, ask'd no vows,
   Nor offer'd any; she had never heard
Of plight and promises to be a spouse,
   Or perils by a loving maid incurr'd;
She was all which pure ignorance allows,
   And flew to her young mate like a young bird;
And, never having dreamt of falsehood, she
Had not one word to say of constancy.

191

She loved, and was beloved—she adored,
   And she was worshipp'd; after nature's fashion,
Their intense souls, into each other pour'd,
   If souls could die, had perish'd in that passion—

But by degrees their senses were restored,
  Again to be o'ercome, again to dash on;
And, beating 'gainst *his* bosom, Haidee's heart
Felt as if never more to beat apart.

192

Alas! they were so young, so beautiful,
  So lonely, loving, helpless, and the hour
Was that in which the heart is always full
  And, having o'er itself no further power,
Prompts deeds eternity can not annul,
  But pays off moments in an endless shower
Of hellfire—all prepared for people giving
Pleasure or pain to one another living.

193

Alas! for Juan and Haidee! they were
  So loving and so lovely—till then never,
Excepting our first parents, such a pair
  Had run the risk of being damn'd forever;
And Haidee, being devout as well as fair,
  Had, doubtless, heard about the Stygian river,
And hell and purgatory—but forgot
Just in the very crisis she should not.

194

They look upon each other, and their eyes
  Gleam in the moonlight; and her white arm clasps
Round Juan's head, and his around her lies
  Half buried in the tresses which it grasps;
She sits upon his knee, and drinks his sighs,
  He hers, until they end in broken gasps;
And thus they form a group that's quite antique,
Half naked, loving, natural, and Greek.

195

And when those deep and burning moments pass'd,
  And Juan sunk to sleep within her arms,
She slept not, but all tenderly, though fast,
  Sustain'd his head upon her bosom's charms;
And now and then her eye to heaven is cast,
  And then on the pale cheek her breast now warms,
Pillow'd on her o'erflowing heart, which pants
With all it granted, and with all it grants.

196

An infant when it gazes on a light,
  A child the moment when it drains the breast,
A devotee when soars the Host in sight,
  An Arab with a stranger for a guest,
A sailor when the prize has struck in fight,
  A miser filling his most hoarded chest,
Feel rapture; but not such true joy are reaping
As they who watch o'er what they love while sleeping.

197

For there it lies so tranquil, so beloved,
  All that it hath of life with us is living;
So gentle, stirless, helpless, and unmoved,
  And all unconscious of the joy 'tis giving;
All it hath felt, inflicted, pass'd, and proved,
  Hush'd into depths beyond the watcher's diving;
There lies the thing we love with all its errors
And all its charms, like death without its terrors.

198

The lady watch'd her lover—and that hour
  Of Love's, and Night's, and Ocean's solitude,
O'erflow'd her soul with their united power;
  Amidst the barren sand and rocks so rude

She and her wave-worn love had made their bower,
  Where naught upon their passion could intrude,
And all the stars that crowded the blue space
Saw nothing happier than her glowing face.

199

Alas! the love of women! it is known
  To be a lovely and a fearful thing;
For all of theirs upon that die is thrown,
  And if 'tis lost, life hath no more to bring
To them but mockeries of the past alone,
  And their revenge is as the tiger's spring,
Deadly, and quick, and crushing; yet, as real
Torture is theirs, what they inflict they feel.

200

They are right; for man, to man so oft unjust,
  Is always so to women; one sole bond
Awaits them, treachery is all their trust;
  Taught to conceal, their bursting hearts despond
Over their idol, till some wealthier lust
  Buys them in marriage—and what rests beyond?
A thankless husband, next a faithless lover,
Then dressing, nursing, praying, and all's over.

201

Some take a lover, some take drams or prayers,
  Some mind their household, others dissipation,
Some run away, and but exchange their cares,
  Losing the advantage of a virtuous station;
Few changes e'er can better their affairs,
  Theirs being an unnatural situation,
From the dull palace to the dirty hovel:
Some play the devil, and then write a novel.

202

Haidee was Nature's bride, and knew not this;
  Haidee was Passion's child, born where the sun
Showers triple light, and scorches even the kiss
  Of his gazelle-eyed daughters; she was one
Made but to love, to feel that she was his
  Who was her chosen: what was said or done
Elsewhere was nothing—She had naught to fear,
Hope, care, nor love beyond, her heart beat *here*.

203

And oh! that quickening of the heart, that beat!
  How much it costs us! yet each rising throb
Is in its cause as its effect so sweet,
  That Wisdom, ever on the watch to rob
Joy of its alchemy, and to repeat
  Fine truths; even Conscience, too, has a tough job
To make us understand each good old maxim,
So good—I wonder Castlereagh don't tax 'em.

204

And now 'twas done—on the lone shore were plighted
  Their hearts; the stars, their nuptial torches, shed
Beauty upon the beautiful they lighted:
  Ocean their witness, and the cave their bed,
By their own feelings hallow'd and united,
  Their priest was Solitude, and they were wed:
And they were happy, for to their young eyes
Each was an angel, and earth paradise.

208

But Juan! had he quite forgotten Julia?
  And should he have forgotten her so soon?
I can't but say it seems to me most truly a
  Perplexing question; but, no doubt, the moon

Does these things for us, and whenever newly a
   Strong palpitation rises, 'tis her boon,
Else how the devil is it that fresh features
Have such a charm for us poor human creatures?

209

I hate inconstancy—I loathe, detest,
   Abhor, condemn, abjure the mortal made
Of such quicksilver clay that in his breast
   No permanent foundation can be laid;
Love, constant love, has been my constant guest,
   And yet last night, being at a masquerade,
I saw the prettiest creature, fresh from Milan,
Which gave me some sensations like a villain.

210

But soon Philosophy came to my aid,
   And whisper'd "think of every sacred tie!"
"I will, my dear Philosophy!" I said,
   "But then her teeth, and then, Oh heaven! her eye!
I'll just inquire if she be wife or maid,
   Or neither—out of curiosity."
"Stop!" cried Philosophy, with air so Grecian,
(Though she was masked then as a fair Venetian).

211

"Stop!" so I stopp'd—But to return: that which
   Men call inconstancy is nothing more
Than admiration due where nature's rich
   Profusion with young beauty covers o'er
Some favor'd object; and as in the niche
   A lovely statue we almost adore,
This sort of adoration of the real
Is but a heightening of the "beau ideal."

212

'Tis the perception of the beautiful,
   A fine extension of the faculties,
Platonic, universal, wonderful,
   Drawn from the stars, and filter'd through the skies,
Without which life would be extremely dull;
   In short, it is the use of our own eyes,
With one or two small senses added, just
To hint that flesh is form'd of fiery dust.

213

Yet 'tis a painful feeling, and unwilling,
   For surely if we always could perceive
In the same object graces quite as killing
   As when she rose upon us like an Eve,
'Twould save us many a heartache, many a shilling,
   (For we must get them anyhow, or grieve)
Whereas if one sole lady pleased forever,
How pleasant for the heart, as well as liver!

216

In the meantime, without proceeding more
   In this anatomy, I've finish'd now
Two hundred and odd stanzas as before,
   That being about the number I'll allow
Each canto of the twelve, or twenty-four;
   And, laying down my pen, I make my bow,
Leaving Don Juan and Haidee to plead
For them and theirs with all who deign to read.

From CANTO III

1

Hail, Muse! *et cetera*—We left Juan sleeping,
　　Pillow'd upon a fair and happy breast,
And watch'd by eyes that never yet knew weeping,
　　And loved by a young heart, too deeply blessed
To feel the poison through her spirit creeping,
　　Or know who rested there; a foe to rest
Had soil'd the current of her sinless years,
And turn'd her pure heart's purest blood to tears.

2

Oh, Love! what is it in this world of ours
　　Which makes it fatal to be loved? Ah why
With cypress branches hast thou wreathed thy bowers,
　　And made thy best interpreter a sigh?
As those who dote on odors pluck the flowers,
　　And place them on their breast—but place to die—
Thus the frail beings we would fondly cherish
Are laid within our bosoms but to perish.

3

In her first passion woman loves her lover,
　　In all the others all she loves is love,
Which grows a habit she can ne'er get over,
　　And fits her loosely—like an easy glove,
As you may find, whene'er you like to prove her:
　　One man alone at first her heart can move;
She then prefers him in the plural number,
Not finding that the additions much encumber.

4

I know not if the fault be men's or theirs;
   But one thing's pretty sure; a woman planted—
(Unless at once she plunge for life in prayers)—
   After a decent time must be gallanted;
Although, no doubt, her first of love affairs
   Is that to which her heart is wholly granted;
Yet there are some, they say, who have had *none*,
But those who have ne'er end with only *one*.

5

'Tis melancholy, and a fearful sign
   Of human frailty, folly, also crime,
That love and marriage rarely can combine,
   Although they both are born in the same clime;
Marriage from love, like vinegar from wine—
   A sad, sour, sober beverage—by time
Is sharpen'd from its high celestial flavor
Down to a very homely household savor.

6

There's something of antipathy, as 'twere,
   Between their present and their future state;
A kind of flattery that's hardly fair
   Is used until the truth arrives too late—
Yet what can people do, except despair?
   The same things change their names at such a rate;
For instance—passion in a lover's glorious,
But in a husband is pronounced uxorious.

7

Men grow ashamed of being so very fond,
   They sometimes also get a little tired
(But that, of course, is rare), and then despond:
   The same things cannot always be admired,

Yet 'tis "so nominated in the bond,"
    That both are tied till one shall have expired.
Sad thought! to lose the spouse that was adorning
Our days, and put one's servants into mourning.

8

There's doubtless something in domestic doings,
    Which forms, in fact, true love's antithesis;
Romances paint at full length people's wooings,
    But only give a bust of marriages;
For no one cares for matrimonial cooings,
    There's nothing wrong in a connubial kiss:
Think you, if Laura had been Petrarch's wife,
He would have written sonnets all his life?

9

All tragedies are finish'd by a death,
    All comedies are ended by a marriage;
The future states of both are left to faith,
    For authors fear description might disparage
The worlds to come of both, or fall beneath,
    And then both worlds would punish their miscarriage;
So leaving each their priest and prayer book ready,
They say no more of Death or of the Lady.

10

The only two that in my recollection
    Have sung of heaven and hell, or marriage, are
Dante and Milton, and of both the affection
    Was hapless in their nuptials, for some bar
Of fault or temper ruin'd the connection
    (Such things, in fact, it don't ask much to mar);
But Dante's Beatrice and Milton's Eve
Were not drawn from their spouses, you conceive.

11

Some persons say that Dante meant theology
By Beatrice, and not a mistress—I,
Although my opinion may require apology,
Deem this a commentator's fantasy,
Unless indeed it was from his own knowledge he
    Decided thus, and show'd good reason why;
I think that Dante's more abstruse ecstatics
Meant to personify the mathematics.

12

Haidée and Juan were not married, but
    The fault was theirs, not mine: it is not fair,
Chaste reader, then, in any way to put
    The blame on me, unless you wish they were;
Then if you'd have them wedded, please to shut
    The book which treats of this erroneous pair,
Before the consequences grow too awful;
'Tis dangerous to read of loves unlawful.

13

Yet they were happy—happy in the illicit
    Indulgence of their innocent desires;
But more imprudent grown with every visit,
    Haidée forgot the island was her sire's;
When we have what we like, 'tis hard to miss it,
    At least in the beginning, ere one tires;
Thus she came often, not a moment losing,
Whilst her piratical papa was cruising.

14

Let not his mode of raising cash seem strange,
    Although he fleeced the flags of every nation,
For into a prime minister but change
    His title, and 'tis nothing but taxation;

But he, more modest, took an humbler range
    Of life, and in an honester vocation
Pursued o'er the high seas his watery journey,
And merely practiced as a sea attorney.

15

The good old gentleman had been detain'd
    By winds and waves, and some important captures;
And, in the hope of more, at sea remain'd,
    Although a squall or two had damp'd his raptures,
By swamping one of the prizes; he had chain'd
    His prisoners, dividing them like chapters
In number'd lots; they all had cuffs and collars,
And averaged each from ten to a hundred dollars.

19

Then having settled his marine affairs,
    Dispatching single cruisers here and there,
His vessel having need of some repairs,
    He shaped his course to where his daughter fair
Continued still her hospitable cares;
    But that part of the coast being shoal and bare,
And rough with reefs which ran out many a mile,
His port lay on the other side o' the isle.

20

And there he went ashore without delay,
    Having no custom house nor quarantine
To ask him awkward questions on the way
    About the time and place where he had been:
He left his ship to be hove down next day,
    With orders to the people to careen;
So that all hands were busy beyond measure,
In getting out goods, ballast, guns, and treasure.

96

But let me to my story: I must own,
    If I have any fault, it is digression;
Leaving my people to proceed alone,
    While I soliloquize beyond expression;
But these are my addresses from the throne,
    Which put off business to the ensuing session:
Forgetting each omission is a loss to
The world, not quite so great as Ariosto.

97

I know that what our neighbors call *"longueurs,"*
    (We've not so good a *word,* but have the *thing*
In that complete perfection which ensures
    An epic from Bob Southey every spring—)
Form not the true temptation which allures
    The reader; but 'twould not be hard to bring
Some fine examples of the *épopée,*
To prove it grand ingredient is *ennui.*

98

We learn from Horace, Homer sometimes sleeps;
    We feel without him: Wordsworth sometimes wakes,
To show with what complacency he creeps,
    With his dear *"Waggoners,"* around his lakes;
He wishes for "a boat" to sail the deeps—
    Of ocean?—No, of air; and then he makes
Another outcry for "a little boat,"
And drivels seas to set it well afloat.

99

If he must fain sweep o'er the ethereal plain,
    And Pegasus runs restive in his "waggon,"
Could he not beg the loan of Charles's Wain?
    Or pray Medea for a single dragon?

Or if too classic for his vulgar brain,
    He fear'd his neck to venture such a nag on,
And he must needs mount nearer to the moon,
Could not the blockhead ask for a balloon?

<h2 style="text-align:center">100</h2>

"Peddlers," and "boats," and "waggons"! Oh! ye shades
    Of Pope and Dryden, are we come to this?
That trash of such sort not alone evades
    Contempt, but from the bathos' vast abyss
Floats scumlike uppermost, and these Jack Cades
    Of sense and song above your graves may hiss—
The "little boatman" and his "Peter Bell"
Can sneer at him who drew "Achitophel"!

<h2 style="text-align:center">101</h2>

T' our tale—The feast was over, the slaves gone,
    The dwarfs and dancing girls had all retired;
The Arab lore and poet's song were done,
    And every sound of revelry expired;
The lady and her lover, left alone,
    The rosy flood of twilight's sky admired—
Ave Maria! o'er the earth and sea,
That heavenliest hour of Heaven is worthiest thee!

<h2 style="text-align:center">102</h2>

Ave Maria! blessed be the hour!
    The time, the clime, the spot, where I so oft
Have felt that moment in its fullest power
    Sink o'er the earth so beautiful and soft,
While swung the deep bell in the distant tower,
    Or the faint dying day-hymn stole aloft,
And not a breath crept through the rosy air,
And yet the forest leaves seem'd stirr'd with prayer.

103

Ave Maria! 'tis the hour of prayer!
Ave Maria! 'tis the hour of love!
Ave Maria! may our spirits dare
    Look up to thine and to thy Son's above!
Ave Maria! oh that face so fair!
    Those downcast eyes beneath the Almighty dove—
What though 'tis but a pictured image strike—
That painting is no idol, 'tis too like.

104

Some kinder casuists are pleased to say,
    In nameless print—that I have no devotion;
But set those persons down with me to pray,
    And you shall see who has the properest notion
Of getting into Heaven the shortest way;
    My altars are the mountains and the ocean,
Earth, air, stars—all that springs from the great Whole,
Who hath produced, and will receive the soul.

INDEX OF TITLES AND FIRST LINES